Table of Contents

Chapter One

"Introduction to the Game"

First off let me explain what a "chilli pimp" is.

A chili pimp is a small time pimp; it is a pimp who will have between one and three girls. He does not stay in the most expensive hotels or eats in the most expensive restaurants; he can't afford to. What he relies on is his ability to give more care, attention and on the spot dependability than a "pimp" can give. All pimps started out as chili-pimps. Some pimps even refer to the stage as the minor leagues. It can also be seen as a make it or break it period in a young pimp's career. A young kid will either develop a "stable" or he will "blow hoeless" and return to the drug or gigolo game. A chilli pimp can either be an amateur or a pimp on his way up.

A chilli pimp could also be a pimp who has become addicted to drugs, and in some strange way the only girl he is left with is the one who really loves him, feels sorry for him, and in her way, has shown that she cares and is willing to continue working the "track" to get him his fix to make him "well." It's her way of mothering him, even though she is nursing him from one dope fiend fix to the next. A chilli pimp can also be an old pimp who is semi-retired and has sold, retired, blown, been peeled or fired most of his stable and settled down with his "bottom" women and maybe her favorite girl who lives with them like a daughter. In this situation, they will let her recruit a girl from time to time to stay with them.

A chilli pimp is never a threat to the established pimp, who actually looks at the chilli pimp, not with contempt but as if they are amused by the chilli pimps. It's kind of like how a father or an uncle who looks at his children or nephew's when they wear his clothes or who are going on their first date. Established pimps are actually flattered because they know that we are trying to imitate them. That is why, while pimps are brutal in their competition with each other, they deal with chilli pimps with "kid" gloves. They will "front" the chilli pimp money, give you advice, and, if one of them takes a liking to you, he might give the chilli pimp one of his girls, if his stable is too large.

You must always be careful though, because pimps are the "masters" of game and will run game on you if nothing else just to test you. An established pimp will see that a chilli pimp has only one girl and will offer him a "rib"; that is, one of his girls whom the chilli pimp will only manage for him but does not own. The two of you will split her "quota", the target number of money she must make in one night. But in actuality, she is just a spy for that pimp, who has either become jealous or threatened because the chilli pimp is starting to rise.

Chilli pimps have to concentrate on his budget more than anything else. While the "real" pimps are driving up and down Atlantic and Pacific Avenue in Bentley and live in the Borgata or Taj Mahal, chilli pimps have to live in the "El Greco" with a small refrigerator, a microwave, two beds (thank God). Hopefully, the pad is on the first floor facing Pacific Avenue where the chilli pimp can at any time walk out and see if his girl is walking home or if there was any "drama" going on the "track". He hass to keep the nicest clothes that his budget will allow

(1) So that his girl will not be embarrassed to call you her man

(2) So that you can possibly attract working girls with the hope that they "choose" you over their current pimp, or that they stop "renegading" and come in out of the cold and have a man.

You must always be able to feed your girl and have bail money. You must let her know that you will find her if you don't hear from her.

As a chillip pimp, I let my girl know that I had all the numbers for the hospitals, emergency rooms, police departments, the morgue, bail bondsmen, and a good New Jersey lawyer who knows the ins and outs to local laws as well as the local prosecutors, and judges.

You do this to let her know you have her back. Most of all, you had to let her know that you are more than willing to do what a pimp does best and that is to protect her. You breakdown the rules to her. Never go on any claimed turf and never look at a pimp in his eyes (that's called reckless eyeballing).

You take a deep breath and hit the track. You're always on top of your budget like a damn bookkeeper. You must always set your quota lower than the local pimps. You make it advantageous for the girl to stay with you, even though that's cheating the pimp rules. It means that if she chooses to chase another pimp, she will have to pay him more and keep less money for herself. After all, someone has to pay for that Bentley. You also try to show her what qualities you have that will set you apart from other pimps. You can, for instance, occasionally tell her to call home and check on her child. You keep a tight reign on her, but you try to make her really believe in you because you are worried about her and "love" her.

My personal touch, was with believe it or not, food. I would take mental notes of her favorite foods while we talked and then do my very best to have, if not that very food, the closest to it one could find in Atlantic City waiting for her at 5:00 a.m. when she turned in. You are to provide her with all the toiletries a woman needs, especially those she needs in her line of work: douches, vaginal spray, an endless supply of condoms, female condoms, Listerine, tooth brushes, bobbie pins, scrunchies, curling irons, etc.

I really went the extra mile when trying to make my girl comfortable; I even had the girls try hydrogen peroxide after being out all night. I told them that it worked better than Listerine and that the evidence was in the bubbles. The more bubbles meant the more germs the hydrogen peroxide was killing. My girls liked it; it made them feel clean. Most importantly, it was a hell of

a lot cheaper than Listerine. Don't forget you have to be able to do all of this at certain times

from one girl's "quota".

Believe me, I never had a dime to spare. Another bonus that helped me get by in Atlantic

City was that in New Jersey you couldn't pump your own gas. You paid after your gas was

pumped. I must have hit every gas station in Atlantic City, Egg Harbor, all the way up Black

Horse Pike and beyond. I hardly paid for gas once while I was there. Of course, my girl didn't

know it. That would have made me look low budget. I always did it when she was working. I'm

sure the "real pimps" have their problems financially, but they are the masters of the "all is well"

routine. As a chilli pimp you score points with your girl for running this routine because she

knows more than anyone else that you are desperate to just make it from one day to the next. If

you make it from the "chilli pimp" faze to the show-nuff pimping faze then, to say the least, you

are tried and true, purified and bona fide, and you have earned the right to be called a PIMP

(WITH CAPITAL LETTERS).

Chapter Two

How I developed the mind and the stomach for the Pimp Game

When I was nine years old, my grandmother, Dorothy English, who we dearly called

"Mudda", moved from my house on 27 Cambridge Place to 130 3rd Avenue in Brooklyn's

Wyckoff Housing Projects. Two blocks away on Douglas Street and 3rd Avenue was the Douglas

Pool and Park. At night time it was mostly a thriving track. I would sit on the mailbox on the southwest corner of the intersection until the wee hours of the night, watching the pimps work

the girls. It was like magic, the control they exercise over them. To me, no one had his shit

together as much as a pimp. The way they dressed, talked, walked, the cars they drove and the

girls they had. I mean, any adult male who chose another profession was a fool. I really felt that

way back then. My curiosity and hunger for knowledge about the game intensified every night

that I watched them. A popular song that captured the way I felt about it at the time was "Brick"

by the Dazz Band.

As the sun went down on 3rd Avenue, a big white Cadillac would pull to the curb across

from the Daily News building. You could hear: "Everybody get up and dance if you want to.....

If the music makes you want to move..... well, alright!"

At first I was in a state of complete lust with the ladies of the night. Their sequence

shorts, bustier tops, spiked heels, blonde wigs, bright layered make-up drove this nine year old

boy crazy. I asked an older man one night (and by older I mean he was about sixteen). "What

does it take to have women like that?" He said "A toot-toot cost two-five and a beat-beat cost

fifty dollars". Although twenty-five dollars for head and fifty dollars for a screw would have

taken a big toll on my "newspaper" money at the time, that was not what I had meant. I wanted

to know what it took to own those women, to possess their very being, just like their pimp did.

Then that very night I saw him; he was everything I wanted to be; and from what I saw, he had

everything I wanted.

At this point, I had been out there every night for two weeks, watching the girls work.

But on this night they were working especially hard, and creating a traffic jam. The cars would

come down 3rd Avenue until they passed the park on that block where the entrances to the pool were they than would make a right turn at the top of the block. Where all the girls congregated; the cars would stop and all the girls would run up to them from both sides. The men or women in the cars would discuss prices and asked what they wanted. It all took less than ten seconds to transact.

The girls would jump into the car in the traffic jam and sit until the cop reached the bottom of the block. Then the girls would jump out of the cars while they counted the money. I noticed that the one woman out there was dressed nicely, but not like a whore, and all the girls seemed to answer to her. Although I had seen her on the "track" before and dressed like a whore, she wasn't dressed like it tonight. She reported to a white Cadillac. I saw her every so often throughout the night go to the white Cadillac and report to the pimp, hand him what I assumed was money and received whatever verbal instructions he gave. I was trying to follow what was going on as hard as I could from the mailbox, but I would have to get closer if I was ever going to learn of this mystical magical power this rarest black man had.

I climbed down off of the mailbox and proceeded to walk South bound on 3rd Avenue. The park was to my right, and I was amazed that people were screwing and getting head jobs right out in the open!!!

Oh man, I thought, this is paradise! Anyway, I told myself: focus man and find out how to be that man in the car. As I got closer, about ten feet away from the car, I saw the "Bottom Women" say "Ya'll don't like working so hard; so don't fuck up daddy's money no more!" I thought: "These bitches done fucked up the pimps' money. So tonight he's out here working them personally, and it looks as though he might work them to death."

I was so amazed by the goings on that I wasn't even standing close to the fence (for those of you not from Brooklyn that means darkness). I just stood there, I wasn't even four feet tall

under the street light, staring at all the ladies of the night darting in between cars, flirting with the

cars as they passed, adjusting their clothes, which were more like costumes, and my personal

favorite, the ladies switching hard doing the "strut" along the traffic jam and making all the

would be customers salivate.

At first I saw the window come down, then the door opened and then "HE" stepped out.

To this day I believe that it was "HE" that I wanted to see. I first noticed how tall he appeared.

He wore a white "Macaroni" hat cocked "Ace Deuce" with a red rooster feather on the side. He

wore a white silk shirt with the collar open reaching his shoulders. The shirt was tucked tightly

into his hip hugging bell bottom white pants that flowed with the breeze on top of his red leather

platform shoes. He had long pinky nails and wore a gold rope chain that was thick, but mind you

not a "cable" like Run DMC thick; they weren't even out yet but maybe an inch or two round.

On the gold chain he wore a gold cross that turned into a spoon at the bottom.

To my surprise he was light skinned like me. In Bed-Stuy Court where I lived, "Piss"

colored niggers were even below dark skinned blacks as far as achievement and self-esteem

went. I looked at him and then noticed he was looking at me. He gave me a sinister fatherly

smile and said, "What's happening young blood?" Then he went back to ordering his women

around. He clapped his hands very loudly, just like in the "Clap on Clap Off" commercial.

On cue, the bottom women went to another car. All the girls went to either of the two

assigned seats; I'm sure then they all disappeared into the night.

I always have wondered if the pimp knew what he did to me that night. He had passed the

game on. Since then, I have always wondered how the game had been passed on to him. I also always wondered if he closed down the track that night because a nine year old boy was standing under the street light looking at him as if I had seen Jesus.

As acts of sexual mayhem were going on all around me, I really felt that night that I had seen into the future. That pimp was me grown up, I knew I would do anything to fulfill this Moses like prophecy I had witnessed that night.

In the 70's, New York City suffered a terrible recession. It seemed everyone was doing bad. I didn't know a single black man who had a job, although I new women who did. Most black men seemed to all be in some form of inebriation all day. They would sit in front of the corner store on milk crates in old "pleated" pants, wearing old "Chuck Taylor" converses with the backs broken down so they could wear them like slippers. The "wife beater" tank top completed the black man's uniform of that era. The only change in attire he might be wearing differently from the day before was the grooming tool in his afro. It was either the red, black and green pick with the sides raised, or the pick with the fist or the "rake" comb like "Shirley" from the TV show "What's Happening".

Black men at the time seemed to all be looking for an escape but I couldn't figure out until. It was hopelessness. I was afraid of ending up like all the other black men in my neighborhood. I was hopelessly afraid of hopelessness that is, until I saw the pimp. He gave me hope. I knew I had to watch him closer so I could learn all that he knew. I wanted to be just like him.

The only way for me to get from my house to my grandmother's house was to walk. I would walk straight up Gates Avenue, make a left on South Oxford, walk down to Fulton Street, make a left in front of the Brooklyn Academy of Music, cross Flatbush Avenue extinction and go through State Street to Third Avenue, then down to the projects. One Friday after school, I saw the Pimp. He was on the corner of State Street and Flatbush Avenue, talking to one of his ladies. I looked at him for as long as I could while keeping a normal pace as I walked by.

About half way through the block, I ducked behind a parked truck. The lady he was talking to gave him a peck on the cheek, and they started down the block toward me. I watched. I planned to cross the street if she made it all the way to me.

This lady was really beautiful. She was wearing afro-puffs; a paisley top tied in a knot above her stomach. Her cut-off jean shorts were washed to create that blue shag around the bottom (very popular back then), and she wore spiked heels. Now to me it's not just the clothes but a women's body and how she moves it that really makes her sexy.

This woman had a killer body. She was perfectly sculpted as if she had been carved out of wood. I loved her thick legs, thighs and calves. Once you have those things all a woman needs to have the perfect body is a really thick ass. Mmmph! I can see her now those shiny legs that she soothed with baby oil (I know because I could smell it from five feet away). Her beautiful dark mahogany complexion was enhanced by a red-tint from being in the sun. Yep! She was a Dime!!

About ten feet away, she turned to go into a brownstone and swayed up the stairs. I didn't even notice that the door was open at a 45° angle and that pretty young lady sitting in a chair on the inside was looking directly at me. I couldn't believe I had not noticed her. After all, she was wearing a bright pink hot shorts* covered in sequence. She said something to the lady that I had watched walking from the corner and then pointed at me. They both motioned me to come over. I felt the kind of shock someone would have if they were watching TV and the nightly news anchorman had started directly talking to them. I began walking to them slowly when the one

standing up said: "come on I ain't got all day." So I (in a cool way) jogged up the stairs and

stopped right about where my face was eye level with her "coochie."

I was just nine, but I knew better than to get close to the door. They were prostitutes, but I

didn't know what they did for personal sexual kicks. I was irresistibly drawn to them, but I didn't

want to get castrated or murdered by some sadistic freak. She said, "My face is up here!" I

looked up but was still drawn to her crotch and legs. I can still smell her vagina now. It smelled

as if it was dirty, sticky and sweet, I licked my lips, I wanted some.

She said, "How olds you boy?"

I said, "Eleven."

"You don't look no more than seven."

I was always tiny and even to the day, I look way younger than I am.

"Ok, I'm nine." I told her.

"That's child abuse, I can't give you none."

I blurted: "I thought anyone could "get" some if their pockets were right."

They both looked at each other in feigned shock and then broke out in laughter, looking

as if they were giving each other a "sister girl" high five.

She said. "I'll tell you what, pretty boy. You get twenty-five dollars together and I'll give

you something you'll never forget." The one sitting down talked; "And if you bring fifty you can

have us both."

Then they broke out laughing again, giving each other another high five. I stood there

deadly serious, amazed that all it took was fifty to have both these women. Still, it didn't make any sense to me. I thought: "What was the pimp paying them and what did it take to own and control them the way he did?"

I said: "I'll get the money, just be ready," I tried to be as firm and manly as possible; I stood erect with a big man demeanor. This brought them to near hysteria. The one sitting down was holding her stomach and wiping away the tears. She was laughing so hard that the tears gave her dark face a glaze as she wiped them. It was as if she had wiped Vaseline over it. I got mad and said, "I'll be back and be wearing those same shorts when I do."

They continued to laugh as if they were watching Richard Pryor do a stand-up routine right there on their stoop. Just then the one sitting down looked to her right, out the window in the second floor. I heard a girl's voice say: "Get the fuck off of me! You want some more, you pay for more."

All of a sudden, the two ladies I was conversing with weren't laughing anymore; their dispositions had become murderous. The one standing up kissed her fingers and placed them on my cheek saying, "see you soon, pretty boy". Then they both disappeared behind the slammed door. I stood there for a moment listening to all the screaming. As it began escalating, I trotted down the stairs, made two lefts pass State Street to Third Avenue and headed for the projects.

I had to wake up at 3:30 a.m. so I could be at Third Avenue and Douglas in front of the Daily News building by 4:00 a.m. Which, I would wait in the shadows to steal newspapers from the back of the Daily News trucks. If my female cousin Bassa couldn't sweet talk the driver into giving us his "extra" newspapers to sell.

I couldn't sleep a wink. (It was also hot as hell and the mosquitoes were feasting on me.) It was bad enough I had to sleep on the floor, since my cousin Bassa got to sleep behind my grandmother in her little hospital issued bed. Usually I was miserable when I slept there but not

tonight. I couldn't stop thinking about that "working girl" and remembering the smell of her

sweet nectar smoothed in baby oil. Throughout the night, I touched my face where she touched

it, I didn't know her name, so in my mind her name became "baby oil". The thought of her made

me feel all fuzzy and warm inside.

I jumped out of bed and got dressed with a whole new sense of purpose. My grandmother

and cousin looked at me curiously, my cousin said: "He ain't dragging his feet this morning

huh." "Come on Bassa let's get the papers." I said, as we walked out into the always smokey

hallway on the ninth floor.

I had different plan this morning. Usually, if the driver didn't give us his "extras", I

would steal them from the back of his truck. Now whether he gave Bassa the papers or not, I was

going to steal the newspapers from the back of the truck because I needed twenty-five dollars for

Baby Oil. If humanly possible, I was going to get fifty for her friend "Pink Shorts" too. I knew I

would have to go hungry at night and didn't care. I need new sneakers terribly and forgot all

about it. I was willing to risk my life, if necessary, to be able to lay naked with "Baby Oil". Just

the thought of it made me dizzy.

But three weeks later, after begging, borrowing and stealing, I still didn't have the

money. I went to sleep depressed every night thinking about how I didn't have the money and

that "Baby Oil" was forgetting me more and more. One Friday, I was making my weekly "trek"

to my grandmother's, walking as usual, down Fourth Avenue to Warren Street and then to the

projects. There was a Chinese restaurant on Fourth Avenue that had four arcade games inside.

One game in particular drew a crowd. And there stood Baby Oil and Pink Shorts watching the action. A crowd of men of all ages behind them seemed more interested in their backsides than in

the game going on. It seemed like every five seconds either Baby Oil or Pink Shorts had to turn

around and scream at the people to stop touching their asses. Two kids about my age were even

slapped.

I jockied for position until I was right behind Baby Oil, I stood a full shoulder head

shorter than her. Her backside seemed huge, I knew I wanted to do something to it and I know it

somehow involved my penis but exactly what I wasn't quite sure. I tapped her on her shoulder

and said, "I almost have the money to buy you." She said, "Little boy, don't fuck with me!"

I couldn't believe it; she didn't even remember me. I continued explaining to her even

though her back was to me. I began talking about the brownstone on State Street, what she was

wearing, anything that could jar her memory.

She turned around and said, "Oh, you still looking for some big girl, huh, pretty boy." I

thanked God that she remembered me. "Well where is it?" she demanded. I told her that I was

still working on the money and that I should have it in a few weeks. She curled up her lips as if

to say, "poor baby", and told me to get back to her as soon as I had it.

I got all giddy and excited and stormed out of the store; I was going to work my ass off

that weekend, knowing I still wouldn't have enough after sustaining myself with potato chips

and fudge rounds and what else during the week. The only time I ate real food then was

lunchtime at Public School 204 where I was bussed to school. But we never got to school in time

for the breakfast, so my usual breakfast at the time was pop rocks, that suited me just fine.

Dinner was usually chocolate chip snaps and a quarter Pepsi. I had to squeeze those things into

my meager budget or I was sure to starve to death. It's a wonder I still have any teeth left.

The day finally came when I had fifty dollars. I brought all my single bills and change to "Russo's Deli" on Greene Avenue and changed it in for two crisp twenty dollar bills and a ten dollar bill. Before I headed to the Wyckoff projects, I went back home, all the while thinking I would be killed or even worse robbed and not have the money for Baby Oil.

I went into the downstairs vestibule of Twenty Seven Cambridge Place and closed the doors on both sides of me. I took a long look at these large bills. I had never seen these denominations. I made sure to make note of the faces and remember the names so that I could sound worldly, like a man of experience, when I spoke to the ladies. I saw Alexander Hamilton and Ulysses Grant for the first time. I headed out toward State Street with the song "No half stepping" by Heatwave playing in my head. I was a boss player now and it was time to go stake my claim.

I knocked boldly on the door. Pink Shorts was sitting exactly where I knew she would. She cracked the door open at that perfect 45 degree angle. She had one hand on the door and the other on the door jam; her legs were spread. Anyone walking by could see that she was a professional lady of leisure. Too bad she liked to wear shorts (they were blue sequence on this particular day), because if she was wearing a dress and no panties you would have a perfect view of her snatch as you walked up the stairs. She said "What the fuck you want little boy?" I wasn't as shocked this time; I figured at this point working girls saw so many men that they just simply couldn't remember us all.

I described the girl I was looking for and was delighted when she said with a sinister grin: "Oh! You want Candy!"

I said her name again to myself just so I could hear myself say it. She screamed

"Candaaaay!!"

She just sat there and then stared at me curiously as we heard Candy coming. I had butterflies in my stomach like a young man would have as he waited on the steps of the home of his prom date. She came to the door fixing her hair, perspiring and said "What's going on?" She looked at me as if I was familiar but couldn't quite place me. I started to explain what it was but she said:

"Oh, Pretty Boy" "What's up?"

"I got fifty dollars," I said.

"You got it on you?"

"Yup"

"Let me see."

I got the feeling I was about to be robbed. I had never even put that scenario in the equation, but I figured that I had worked so hard for this money I might as well get robbed trying to buy what I really wanted. What that was, I wasn't exactly sure. But I had caught Candy's attention, so the money was being spent well already. If Candy robbed me, I figured the money was for her anyway, and, believe it or not, I wanted her to have it. So I said, "I'll give it to you once the three of us are inside and undressed."

They both looked at each other, dumb founded. Then they looked at me. Candy said: "How old are you?"

"I told you that before," I said. "I don't have to explain anything anymore because I had fifty dollars."

She looked at me as if to say, "Ok little smart ass, I'm going to take you to school." Then all of a sudden she looked like she felt guilty for even entertaining the thought.

"I can't do it"

"What?"

"You're a little boy; I wouldn't be able to live with myself"

"Why not, I demanded"

"I couldn't fuck a little boy. That's a crime as it should be."

She looked at me like a hunter taking pity on a baby lion. She said, "I can't, if you want the money. Chocolate "go ahead; I just can't," Candy said to her friend and went back inside.

I stood there looking at Chocolate who looked me over as she licked her lips in deep thought. Then she advised me, "Find a girl your own age, talk to her and find out what she really wants, or better yet, needs. Tell her you can give it to her if she would lay with you naked and let you touch or do with her whatever you want."

I said: "What about you? Don't you want the money?" She looked at me with more pity and said, "I do but you're so little I might kill you." I was kind of confused. I understood kindness; It was rare in Brooklyn. But mercy was something that was even rarer.

She took one last look at me and said, "Enjoy yourself; some little helper out there will take your fifty dollars. Now get lost before you get us shut down".

I tried to talk again but she just got annoyed and said "BYE!" while slamming the door in my face. I was pissed then but today, I would find these two ladies and thank them. I would tell them I would have preferred to lose my virginity to both of you, but I got something even more valuable: a clean bill of health and the knowledge that working girls are not just vicious, malicious, money making machines. They are people; they are women who make the most out of a bad situation. They try to survive from day to day in a brutal cold world, just like most black people.

I really thought that if I lost my virginity to those two women I would somehow learn to harness the magic that their pimp possessed. Since that was not going to happen, I would have to settle for watching from afar.

I must admit that it made me feel special when at 4:00 a.m. in the morning, while going to steal our newspapers to sell, I would say to them: "What's up Chocolate?" and "How you feeling Candy?" From all the other young guys trying to steal newspapers from the backs of the delivery trucks and from my cousin, Bassa, I got a look of admiration and jealousy. You see, everybody saw the pimps and prostitutes but no one ever spoke to them. It was kind of as if they were a different breed. People; people would just look at them with curiosity, jealousy and fear, but I was now interacting with them. So it started to appear as if I was somehow connected to the game.

At this point, I wasn't really watching the ladies; I was watching the pimps. The pimps seemed to have come to some type of understanding over what part of the block belong to whom at what time of night. They would transfer the block to one pimp or another and generally share power. I tried really hard to follow how the pimps interacted with each other. Candy and Chocolate's pimp, "My Idol," was my favorite study. At night my cousin, Trent and I would walk to the bodega and pick a pickled pig's foot from the jar and a chic-o-stick, go back to the mailbox on the corner of Douglas Street and Third Avenue and watch the show. I tried to get everything down. I tried to walk like my idol, talk like him, use body language like him, make facial expressions like him, I even told my cousin I would dress like him one day.

That summer was one to remember. It ended tragically with a car accident that killed my cousin, Bassa, and two other cousins. Although I would stay at my grandmother's from time to time, I couldn't run my newspaper hustle anymore; I just couldn't by myself. My cousin Bassa had come up with the hustle, and if I continued to do it without her, I felt as though I was somehow violating or player hating. So I let it die with her out of respect.

About a year later I walking my usual route to my grandmother's on a sunny spring day when I saw my idol on the corner of State Street and Flatbush Avenue, he was very animated, yelling at a young prostitute that I had never seen before. I could tell she was no more than thirteen. He was dressed very nicely, I noticed, but I also noticed something else. He had a towel wrapped around his left arm and his arm was swollen so badly it looked like Popeye's. He was furious, sweating and waving his arms all over the place. He looked at me and changed his disposition somewhat, I guess it was the most he could do under the circumstances. He said: "I ain't seen you in a while, young blood. What happened? You give up on the pimp game?"

He didn't expect an answer. It was a rhetorical question without a pause. He said "Your friends are down the block. They just shut us down." I hurried down the block as if the girls belonged to me or there was something I could do.

I got there just in time to see about eight girls in cuffs, Candy and Chocolate included, being escorted to a van.

In one year they had aged about 15 years. They also looked as if they had been banging dope. They were dried out, their faces sunken in, hair and nails unkept and crusty, and they stunk. On the ground in the front of the house, there were about 10 mattresses piled on top of one another. I walked pass and made eye contact with Candy. There were a lot of cops there, so I swiftly walked by them. I crossed the street and stared for a little bit then before continuing up

the street. Then I crossed over to walk pass them again.

The cop said, "You know someone here kid?" I said "no." I looked at Candy straight in

her eye and walked pass slowly as they all stood there hand-cuffed. I strained to smell some baby

oil but didn't. I kept on walking and didn't look back; I never saw any of them again.

Chapter Three

"Crack Pimpin"

Between '80-'83, crack didn't exist; its predecessor "Base" cocaine was the shit on the street. The best endorsement crack could have had was Richard Pryor burning himself up because of it. It seemed to make everyone curious, everyone except me, that is. Not many people know how to cook base, but my uncle Michael Buie sure did. People in the neighborhood would bring their cocaine to him to cook. I first watched him cook it on the first floor of 27 Cambridge Place before my grandmother moved to the Wyckoff Projects.

After that, I would see him cook it at the Atlantic Terminal Prospect building were he lived on the 30th floor. I tried my best to pay attention as he placed the powder and baking soda in a small mayonnaise jar, and then place it in a pot of boiling water. He used other ingredients as well, but that's very vague in my mind now. Like I said, it was base and not crack. Old school "base heads" still prefer it to crack. They claim crack has chemicals in it that are bad for you, that it gives you pock marks on your face, rots your teeth and destroys your stamina. Go figure "base heads" being selective.

Contrary to popular belief, I believe that crack was the great "equalizer." Until then only the meanest cold-blooded pimps could make money on the streets and only the hardest, most vicious gangstas could make drug money on the streets. I mean a man's game had to be tough to turn a girl out and have her sell her body. As far as the drug game went, if you were not born into it or grew up in a house with it lying on your kitchen table, you had to be hand picked and groomed by older drug dealers who schooled and properly trained for the day you could be one of the top notch smack-men in your neighborhood.

Crack changed all of that. Not only did it give the ordinary Joe the ability to make ten times more than a brain surgeons salary, it made it possible for the average Joe to sleep with beautiful women. The best thing, as far as I'm concerned that crack did was made possible for all eleven and twelve year old boys to sleep with grown women. Believe you me, I took full advantage of it!

The trick was to catch a women when she "bensed" for the first time. You see, a woman will take it occasionally at a family BBQ, local house parties and so forth, but after a few weeks or months of getting "chippy", she will "bense." That meant she was on a mission! When someone is on a mission they will be up for days scoring crack day after day. They can't get high enough. After a few days, of this they usually crash and sleep for days. They come back home to their families and conjure up a big story that makes everyone raise an eyebrow and say: "Why shouldn't we believe her? This never happened before."

Then everyone puts it behind them and tries to give her the benefit of the doubt. But deep inside, her loved ones know something is wrong. Everybody in her family is hard working or is busy at their career, so how would they know that she is out on the block at 4:00 a.m. when only the drug dealers, working girls and addicts are out? No one she knows knows except me. At the point the woman is still "fresh", meaning she hasn't been selling herself to everybody in the neighborhood, she also still resembles herself and not a crack head; she is still basically well kept.

When people take the leap from recreational user to abuser, they tell themselves they will only do it on special occasions. Then they say they will only do it on weekends, then after work, then at lunchtime, then before work, lunchtime and after work, then all the time. That means fuck everything, 'but I gotta get high.'

I had a new hustle, but it was not nearly as good as the newspaper hustle. It was packing bags for customers at the Key Food on Clinton and Green Avenue. With my extra money I set out to lose my virginity to a grown woman in my neighborhood. I would hang around the train station on St. James and Fulton Street and see women coming home from work. A lot of them would buy "base" right on that corner.

"Hey, Ms. Jones, How you feeling?

"I'm fine, Michael. What are you doin' here?

"Just walking home, need some company?"

"Sure, but I got to make a stop first."

"For what?"

When a woman is becoming a base head, she thinks that no one knows it. So she looks insulted, shocked, surprised and says, "You got a lot of damn nerve, little boy!" But before she could continue cursing me out, I would cut her off. "It's alright, Ms. Jones. Nobody knows but me. And besides, I was only saying it because this time it's going to be on me."

"And why would that be?" she said

"Because I think you're beautiful, and I want to get to know you better."

"How old are you now Michael?"

"Eleven"

"Boy I'm old enough to be your mother, and you probably only shoot hot cider anyway," she said.

I shot back: "Well, just make it shoot and you'll get twenty dollars for your trouble."

As we walked up to the tenement on Grand and Putnam Avenues to score, I told her to start walking on Fulton Street toward Second Cambridge Place and wait in front of the record store. As I turned to cop the rock, the men on the corner said: "Check the little man out. He's coppin' so he can get some of that grown tail. Go-ahead little man, just don't smoke none of that shit yourself."

I gave a nod at them and took off with my "ticket" to catch up with her. As we walked down Cambridge Place toward Gates Avenue, she was silent; I could tell she was nervous. As we made a right turn onto Gates Avenue, she said, "I can't believe I'm doing this. I could go to jail for this, Michael. You better not tell anybody".

I said, "Don't worry Ms. Jones, it's just between us".

As we walked up the steps to her house, she nervously fumbled for her keys. A few of her neighbors looked at us curiously. I was clearly a kid, and she was a grown woman dressed like your typical Wall Street woman. Back in those days a Wall Street woman would wear business attire with sneakers. They carried their shoes in their large pocketbooks and changed only at the office.

"Have a seat on the couch, Michael," she said, as she leafed through her mail in the foyer. She then proceeded to her bedroom in the back. I sat on her couch trying my damndest to stay cool. She came out wearing a white terry cloth robe and carried a stem in her hand.

She said, "Where is it?"

"What?" I asked.

"The base, little nigger."

I knew I had to stand firm with this. If I gave it to her first, no way were we having sex. She then tried to get slick, "base head slick". She opened her robe revealing her sweet chocolate body. "Let me smoke it while you touch on me," she soothed.

At this point I got firm, I would not let go of the base until I had sex with this woman. I bawled it up in my left hand and let my right arm hang free in case I had to fight her for it. She looked down at my left hand and took a deep swallow, her lips were twitching, I knew she needed it bad. She tried again. "I didn't even wash," she said. "If you let me smoke it I can relax, take a shower and take my time pleasing you."

I know that even as a grown man that shit sounds real good but you, the reader, and I both know that back then that was pure base head treachery. "I like it funky," I told her, not knowing the difference between clean and dirty twat. The truth is I had never had any twat, period.

"You fucked up Mike?"

"Whatever."

She threw off her robe and shooed me out of her way. I stood up. She plopped down on the couch, put her arms under her legs and lifted them straight up while bending them. She looked as though she was trying to put each knee to each ear. I stood in front of her, flabbergasted. I could not believe that this drug was so powerful that it could make it possible for me, an eleven year old kid, to make a respectable women my mother's age submit to such a position, I felt so strong.

"Go ahead Get it," I commanded, it's yours.

It didn't even dawn on me that I did not know what to do, so I told her I did not. She just smiled and said, "Pull your dick out and stick it in. I know you can see where to put it".

I sure could. She was positioned like a woman posing for "black tail" magazine. She even used her fingers to spread the lips. I pulled out my meat, came toward her to put it to her vaginal lips, closed my eyes and thrusted forward. I opened my eyes and was shocked; I could not believe my face was so close to hers. I was looking square into her eyes and our noses were almost touching. I guessed that was the point of it. I lifted one hand to touch her titty and couldn't believe how soft it was.

"So this is what a titty feels like," I said to myself. I felt her vagina becoming increasingly wet. I felt compelled to kiss her, so I tried. She held her mouth closed and firm. So I laid my head against the side of her head with my face almost touching the wall.

She then said with a very irritate tone, "Michael are we going to fuck or what?" I said, "I thought we were."

She said, "Michael you're a virgin." I sheepishly said, "Yes".

"You gotta hump like when people dance. It has to go in and out.

" She placed her hands on my waist and moved me accordingly. I felt her getting very wet down there. She started making strange faces, even rolling her eyes, as if it felt good. I felt nothing. I tried to get into it and feel what she was feeling, but my penis was just numb. I started to stroke hard and she let my waist go and put her arms around me and held me tightly. That felt really good. I felt like a man. Then something happened that I didn't expect. She started crying.

I stopped immediately; she put hand over her face and turned her head. She couldn't even look at me; I placed the drug in her hand and went to the door. I looked back and she was lighting up the "stem" with tears running down her cheeks. I came down stairs, thinking, "Well, at least I'm not a virgin anymore." I walked around the corner and on to my block. You could hear the latest song out everywhere from cars, from boom boxes, from people's homes: "White Lines" from Grandmaster Flash and the Furious Five. It was a song highly indicative of the times.

A few weeks went, I would see her coming up out of the train station, but she avoided eye contact with me while she rushed home. I knew she was wondering if I had told anyone. But I had not. In Brooklyn, keeping your mouth shut is like the golden rule. If something good was going on in your life, you did not tell anyone because someone would find a way to ruin it. If they could not ruin it by telling the whole neighborhood, they would tell the police or even do something physical to you. Brooklyn is the home of the player hater.

For the time being, I figured that she would try to handle her habit as best as she could with her own money, and since sex with her was not the mind blowing experience, I thought it would be, I was in no rush to pay her for sex again.

One day after a full day at school and an exhausting 4 or 5 hours of packing bags at Key Food, I was sitting on my stoop relaxing with a soda and cookies when I looked up and saw Ms. Jones walking down the street toward my house. She made eye contact with me with a firm, intense stare. I thought she was pissed and might want to fight or something but she winked at me. She did not stop in front of my house. Instead she walked pass, motioning me to follow her but to be inconspicuous. I followed about 10 feet behind her. She did not turn around once. When we got to her house, she just went upstairs and left the door open. Of course, I fell over, not knowing what really to expect, but I was damn I was sure going to find out what she wanted.

I walked into the parlor floor apartment just as before and made myself comfortable on the couch just as before. I heard her in the backroom disrobing. She came just as before, dressed in a white terry cloth robe. I know I had to tell her the truth before it went go any further.

"Ah Ms. Jones, ah….I don't have any money."

She looked like she had just been told there was no Jesus. She implored, "Come on, don't do this to me baby. I'll make it good this time. You could kiss me and everything." I reiterated that I didn't have a dime and that I was very sorry I wasted her time. I turned to leave. She said, "Then you can help me then because I can trust you to keep your mouth shut."

That's the basic connection between pimp and prostitute "TRUST". The trust that everything said or experienced will be held in confidence. The trust that you, the pimp, will not judge or look at her with scorn.

I said, "Sure Ms. Jones what do you want me to do?"

"You know Mr. Morris from your block don't you?" she said, I told her that I did. "He's been hitting on me for years and I always blow him off. I want you to let him know that I'm available but for a fee. I don't want you to make me sound sleazy. If he tells anybody, you just say you were fucking with him and I knew nothing about it".

I held a stone face and simply asked, "How much?"

"Tell him fifty. If he argues, don't go below 35."

Just as I was thinking to myself that I was going to just low ball and ask for the thirty-five dollars, she said to me, as if reading my mind: "Just remember the more I get the more you get."

It had never occurred to me that I would get anything at all, and I had never played the procurer for a sex for money transaction before, except for myself when I attempted to trick

Candy and Chocolate but had failed. I figured that I had to try; it was sure easier than packing

grocery bags at Key Food. If by some act of God it happened multiple times, I might even be

able to eat the elite ghetto meal of four chicken wings and fried rice. Yep, I had to try.

She then continued with instructions. "Bring him here, don't send him here."

"OK," I said, as I hurried off to Mr. Morris' house.

(I rang his bell and his wife answered.)

"Hello, Michael, what brings you here?"

"Is Mr. Morris home?"

"Yes, wait one minute, I'll get him. Is everything alright?"

"Just fine Mrs. Morris. I saw him outside a little while ago and was wondering if he

wanted me to bring him something back from the store. I'm heading there now."

I know it was corny and obviously it didn't make much sense, but it was the best I could

come up with at the time.

"Sure, wait one minute". She gave me a confused and suspicious look and went into the

house to get him.

"Hey Mike, what's going on."

"I need to ask you something: Can you come out to the sidewalk?"

When he came out to the sidewalk, I motioned for him to walk with me.

"Mike what's this about?" he said.

"I heard you were interested in Ms. Jones."

"Who told you that?"

"Don't worry about that kind of stuff, Mike. That's grown folks stuff. When you get to be my age, you will understand."

I calmly listened to him rant about the birds and the bees before I said, "Are you interested or not?"

"What are you saying, Mike?"

"That I can make it happen."

"Make what happen?" he said.

"You know." I made a circle with my left index finger and thumb and stuck my right index finger through it.

He twisted his lips and looked at me as if I had just told him I that I could fly. He burst out laughing.

"How you gonna do that Mike?" he said.

"By paying her!"

He burst out laughing again.

"No…….. you are," I said.

Then he stopped laughing and said, "I'll be God damned, little Michael, you're serious!"

"As cancer," I said.

"She sent you here?"

"Yup."

"She's at home now?"

"Yup."

"How much she want?"

"Fifty dollars."

He scratched his chin, squinted his eyes and let his mind begin to race.

"Do I pay you or her?"

I said, "I guess it's her pussy."

"No it isn't hers, I said. That pussy belongs to whoever is supplying the base head with

base. If I give the money to her and not you, you won't get a dime."

I though about it for a minute and said, "So here's the deal Mr. Morris. You will give me

five dollars and I'll tell her that all you have is forty-five and you hand that to her."

"Solid," he said with a sly smile.

Off we went to Ms. Jones' house, but she was not there. Mr. Morris looked at me as if to

say I had better not be playing some silly game or setting him up to get robbed. I assured him

that she was developing a bad "Jones" so she couldn't sit still long.

"She'll be right back," I said. I sure hoped she would. I was starving and could just taste

the chicken wings and pork fried rice. I would have a soda, too! He had already given me the

five dollars and I was already trying to figure out how to separate myself from him and the five

dollars if she did not show up. After about fifteen minutes, she strolled up to the stop. She had a

gleam in her eye and looked euphoric.

"Michael I've been doing my homework on you," she said. "How come you ain't tell me

that your family and little friends call you Mick-Man"

She turned to Morris. "Mr. Morris, don't be shy now just because my little partner in

crime is here."

Mr. Morris and I sat silent and still on the stoop. We had never saw Ms. Jones like this

before. She was obviously high and talking like a street woman. She noticed how we were looking at her and switched pass us up the stairs. We both admired her beauty as she went by and to the top of the stairs. She turned around to look down at us and said: "Well you coming or not?"

"Mike is coming too?" Mr. Morris said confused and with contempt.

"Of course he is." She looked at me and winked, "He practically lives here." Mr. Morris looked at me incredulously. When she turned to go inside, Morris gave me a little nudge with his elbow. "You pimpin' little motherfucker," he whispered.

Mr. Morris instinctively sat on the couch in the parlor; I stood in the doorway. Ms. Jones had already gone to the back and was taking a quick shower. We both waited silently. Then I heard: "Mick-man come back here." It was my first time in her bedroom. It was very nice, nicer looking than any bedroom that I had ever seen. She had an expensive looking throw rug and a king sized dack wood bed that had all kinds of intricately detailed carvings on it. Huge mirrors on every wall outlined in the same kind of wood that the bed was made out of and a large dresser with a closet that connect to it. Yeah, at that point that was the plushest bedroom I had ever seen.

"Listen Mick-man", she whispered.

"How much you charge him?"

"All he had was forty-five", I whispered back.

"Well where is it, nigger?"

"He got it," I said. I was glad at that point that he did because if I had handed it to her at this point she would have somehow found a way not to go through with it, leaving me to deal with Mr. Morris.

She looked at me firmly and said, "Alright, you stay here in my room. Here take this."

She handed me a Louisville Slugger baseball bat and said: "If you hear me scream come

and knock this mother fucker out.......ok sweetness?"

She gave me a kiss on the cheek and said, "Call me Nobi." She winked at me as she

turned to leave, pointed to the wall and whispered, "You can peek through here if you want."

Other than looking at some "WHT" or some Hustler magazines that I had seen, I had never saw

two people screwing before. I figured it was a good way as any, especially if I was to tangle with

Nobi again.

Mr. Morris sure got his money's worth because they grunted, groaned, screamed,

hollered, slapped, bit, changed positions what looked like a dozen times, sweated, scratched and

pulled hair for what seemed like an hour. I remember thinking to myself, "If that's what I was

suppose to do when we did it, no wonder she rolled her eyes and started crying." As the trick

finished putting his clothes back on he tried to give her a kiss.

"Nigger, back the fuck up off me! Nobi shouted. I got mine you got yours. Now get the

fuck out."

He shouted, "Bitch I'll slap the shit out of you!"

I knew I had to come out now. I was scared of Mr. Morris, even if I had a bat. I probably

would have been scared even if I had a gun. I decided to come out without the bat. He was

pointing his finger in her face when I walked in.

"Mr. Morris! I don't think all that is necessary," I implored. There is really no need for

Mrs. Morris to find out about this. Think of all the kids you got at home."

He paused and looked at me real hard, "You lucky you ain't try to strong arm me boy, I woulda whooped yo' little ass!"

"Like I said Mr. Morris, all of that isn't necessary".

He turned quickly and left. To this day I don't understand what upset him so.

Nobi didn't even bother to rinse her mouth. She said: "Mick-man come with me to Putnam Avenue." She was standing in front of me butt-naked.

I said, "Like that?"

"Oh, let me throw something on." We were out of the house in less than three minutes and practically running to Putnam Avenue. On the way up Grand Avenue we ran into my good friend "Rabbit." He said, "What you headed up there for, Mick-man?"

"Takin' care of some business that's all," I said.

"I see you havin' fun," he said to me, motioning toward Nobi.

"It ain't like that; she's a friend of the family. Tell your sister Jo-Ann I said hello." I had always had a crush on Jo-Ann.

"I'll do that. Be careful Mick-man."

"Later Rabbit"

Nobi laid back and I scored. Then I stared heading toward the Chinese restaurant. "Mick-man, I'm headed back to the house; I'll see you soon, O.K.," Nobi said. The food tasted delicious, I had worked my ass off for that five dollars.

I figured I was done with Nobi after that. She had asked for help and I had given it. I did not go over to her house the next day. So she came looking for me. I did not realize that I was unknowingly running a "Pratt" game on her, which in simple terms, means hard to get. I had gotten what I wanted out of her (loosing my virginity) and getting dinner out of her was too hard for God sakes. Packing people's grocery bags was easier than all that had transpired the day

before. I had even almost got my ass kicked by a grown man.

The next day immediately after school and before I went to Key Foods, I watched the

usual on television; back to back episodes of "Good Times." My sister Shana comes in and says,

"Pat is outside asking for you." Pat and Shareen Calhoun were our childhood friends who lived

down the block. I went outside. Pat told me that Ms. Jones was waiting for me around the corner.

She really needed my help. I felt bad for her. There was nothing in it for me, but I went anyway.

Nobi was patiently waiting for me. She didn't look desperate, so I figured she had just

finished getting high. "I missed you baby," she said softly. I looked at her. Where the hell is this

coming from? She had never spoken like this before.

"It's getting late and I'm scared, can you walk me home?" Mind you this woman was a

head taller than me. I said, half annoyed "Sure, I can do that."

When we got to her house, I was surprised to find four chicken wings and fried rice

sitting on a tray in the living room. I immediately sat down and devoured it. I was not worried

about not showing up at Key Foods. Because I did not get a salary, my only pay was tips. As I

ate, she showered and put on her robe. I was not interested in trying sex again because the first

time left a lot to be desired.

"Come and sit on the bed with me, Mr. Mick-Man," Nobi said, patting the bed. I came

over and sat down.

She said, "Can I have a kiss?"

We kissed slowly and passionately. I was going on 12 and a kiss never made me feel like

that before. I was tingling all over. She started kissing all over my face, nibbling and kissing my ear and undressing me. It felt so good that I could not move. Her hands moved with expert precision, I still do not know how she did it but I was completely naked in no time. She let her robe drop down around her revealing her awesome oiled, shiny, dark chocolate body. She looked something like the tennis star Serena Williams.

"You seem tense baby," Nobi said. "Let me give you a massage."

"O.K.," I said, being unaware of what being tense felt like or that a massage was the cure for tenseness. She began kissing my neck and licking my ears while massaging my back. Then she licked and kissed my whole back. She turned me over and gave me a complete frontal tongue bath from head to toe.

She was wrong about that taking my tenseness away. I was so tense now that I was about to faint. Then she mounted me. My penis didn't feel numb like before. Maybe my body had matured a little. Whatever the case, I could not keep my eyes open. She kissed and licked me ferociously while riding and thrusting me hard.

All of a sudden, I felt like a volcano has erupted inside of me. Every fiber of my body was tingling. All of the hairs on my body were standing on end. She clasped her hands with mine and held them both down on the bed. My whole body spasmed like someone having an epileptic seizure. Then the flood gates opened and I exploded inside of her.

Her mission was accomplished, but she needed my help to get her drugs, so she became my drug. Nobi did not have to worry about looking for me after that. I stay on her ass. She always had me go find and procure a sexual deal. After school each day, I would secure between two and three tricks. I cut my way up to ten dollars a trick. I was getting thirty dollars a day and on the weekend at least fifty a day. I was eating well and even growing a little bit. I even worked it out so she did not have to go to the drug spot anymore. She loved that. Each night after she

was finished with the tricks, she took me to school. I never imagined that sex could be so

complex: We used all kinds of positions. She made sure I knew the best ones to stimulate the

clitoris more intensely.

School was an entirely different situation though. I was attending Satelite East Junior

High School (also known as P.S. 3) on Franklin and Jefferson Avenue. After dealing with Nobi, I

had a very hard time dealing with girls my own age. I had the biggest crush on Monica Franklin

was one of my classmates, but knew that we were not on the same level. By that I mean maturity

wise. To her a tongue kiss was a big deal. Meanwhile, Nobi was teaching me ejaculation control.

Since I was having a hard time with the girls my age, I started asking Nobi for advice and I

received a treasure chest of information.

I had a large group of friends at this time, but my closest friends were Wesley Trapp and

Glenn Horton. We were like brothers. Wesley was born to parents from Belize and Glenn's

father was from Barbados. People from countries that were once under British control had a

certain type of sternness about them. Self-control, discipline, controlling your emotions and

above all dignity use your attributes. These people did not believe in begging, which was a stark

contrast to my upbringing of African Americans who are use to living on their needs. From

hanging around, my two best friends, I adopted their foreign ways. Monica helped me with

women. I never seemed too eager or anxious with Nobi. I always maintained my self-control and

that seemed to really light her fire. You see a man with self-control usually never reduces

himself to being a "trick."

As I finessed information from Nobi about how to deal with girls my own age, I never seemed too eager to get the answers. By acting this way, I got all the answers I wanted and then some.

I let Nobi know that there was a certain girl on my block that I was really sexually interested in. I told Nobi I was stumped. The girl was much bigger than me and did not seem interested in having sex with me, although she was a good friend. In our large group of friends we had played 'spin the bottle' and 'truth or dare' together, so we had kissed and what not, but I wanted to own her like I did Nobi, meaning I wanted power over her. Nobi let me know that everybody has a sweet tooth. To find out what it is aching for and provide it.

I started hanging around this girl's house and speaking to her whenever I could, looking for her sweet tooth. We talked for days and days, I was prodding in every direction, looking for the angle into her panties, when one afternoon, while she and I were on her couch talking, she said, "Look at my sneakers, they are a mess." I looked down and saw her busted black swede on white leather Pumas. "I need some new kicks bad, I would kill for some Stan Smith Adidas."

Although I was getting good money from Nobi at this time, I was putting it all to good use. By good use, I mean Izod shirts, Lee jeans, Kangol hats and all the proper trimmings for a young man in 1983. To put it plain, in those days Stan Smith Adidas were a steep request. So I decided that if I was going to have to trick, I was going to trick with someone else's money.

I approached my friend Glenn about my idea, not because I knew he had the money from working his ass off at Russo's Deli after school, but because he and I both had a crush on her. We would watch her house from his with a pair of binoculars, hoping to get a glimpse of her in a slip or something tantalizing like that. I knew how bad Glenn wanted her. I also knew he was a virgin.

One afternoon when we knew she was home alone we rang the bell. "Glenn calm down," I said. "She'll go for it believe me." I told Glenn he had a look of a deer caught in the headlights.

"Nigger, you crazy," Glenn said. "She ain't gonna fuck us for no sneaker money. Besides I don't have the full amount!"

I said, "Just be cool. We ain't gonna just run at her like thoroughbreds at the sound of the gun. We gonna finesse her."

She invited us to her kitchen and offered something to drink. We made small conversation and watched TV until I decided it was time.

"Hey girl!" I said cheerfully. "Remember you were telling me how badly you wanted those Stan Smith Adidas? Well I found out a way for you to get them."

She said, "Really! How?"

"Me and my boy Glenn want to spend sometime with you. Alone and separate. As my friend Glenn looked very nervous but he maintained his cool, composed himself and fixed a hard stare, just like one you need in a situation like this. An icy cold stare is really the only thing a young chicken-head respects in conversation besides a swift kick in her ass.

"I don't know Mick-man."

"You crazy!" She stared for a moment and said, "You're serious?"

I said, "Yeah, ain't nobody got to know. You get what you want and we get what we want, and no one is the wiser."

She stared at both of us for a moment than said, "How much money and where is it?"

I motioned to Glenn and he put thirty-two dollars on the table. She looked at us and said,

"With tax, Stan Smith's cost forty-one dollars and that's suppose to be for both of ya'll?"

She felt as if it was bad enough that we had got her to consider screwing us for money, but now we didn't even have the amount that we offered to pay. I sprang into action. "Come on, give us some time. We'll get the rest of it."

"What do you mean we?" she said. "Glenn's the only one here who's gonna get some pussy because he's the only one who's paying."

For the first time Glenn spoke up. "You got my word you'll get the rest of the money. But this was my man's idea. If he don't get none we don't have a deal." We needed to seal the deal. Glenn reached into his pocket and pulled out a bottle of emotion lotion. I had heard her mention several times during our conversations that she wanted to try some, but Glenn was the one who acted on it. He placed a full bottle on top of the money. We hoped that would seal the deal. She nodded in agreement said, "Come on Glenn, you're going first." I grinded my teeth with disgust knowing I would get sloppy seconds but I figured, hey, it's free; get in where you fit in.

She led Glenn into her laundry room; told me to make myself comfortable and wait my turn. I wasn't even half way through watching "Jeopardy" "MTV" when Glenn came out with his big smile on his face saying, "Good idea man, Good idea." Nobi came out and looked at me with a smile. She said, "Let me freshen up a bit." She disappeared into her laundry room. I could hear the water running. Thank God, I thought, that I do not believe in running up in a woman that had just got through screwing another man so all this planning would have been moot. Although for that era "running trains", "gang banging" and all that group sex stuff was the norm for twelve year old boys. It was never my thing. The thought of being next to another man's bodily fluids made my skin crawl and still does. So I peeked in on her as she washed up. I saw her using

something that looked like a turkey baster to flush out her vagina. I had waited so long and had

such a crush on her that when she came out to get me and lead me to her bathroom in the back of

her basement, I might as well have been on vacation with her on a tropical island. Time seemed

to stand still in that tiny bathroom. I was so much shorter than her that she had to bend her knees

a great deal for us to do it standing, doggy style.

Glenn and I really used our heads after that one. We never paid her what we owed her,

although we did pay her again. We told her that we would tell everyone on our block that she had

sold herself to us if she didn't continue to screw us from time to time. In essence, we agreed to

share her, although I always thought she was closer to Glenn. After a while those two were like

best friends, I would get a quickie after school from time to time while those two seemed to fuck

all the time. She turned out to be more experienced than I thought. I learned from her that lying

to a woman and omitting what you're about are two different things. So I figured that when it

comes to women, let them know what you're really all about and don't be afraid of being told to

go to hell. Who knows; she might be on her way to hell too and in need of a ride.

I became very straight forward and cocky after my conquest of the girl on my block. I

thought that every girl had a price or had a secret that could be used against her. So when I was

cutting class in the Satellite East hallway and saw Kelly Kotero cutting class as well. I thought

she would never tell that I slapped her on her ass because after all she was cutting class, right?

Boy was I wrong; I was hauled into the principal's office like Public Enemy #1. After

being read the riot act and apologizing excessively to Kelly, I was cut loose with a warning. My

Spanish teacher who also lived upstairs from me made it her business to talk to my parents about it. My parents, with whom I had never had anything in common, went completely off the handle.

At this point, I figured I did not need them anyway. I had Nobi. She was my bitch, was she not?

So, why the fuck am I staying here? It had not even occurred to me that I had not seen Nobi in a

few days due to all the drama surrounding Kelly Kotero's ass.

The next day, I ran away from home. Actually, I just ran around the corner to Nobi's

house one block away, but she was gone. I felt so stupid. She had been turning tricks; she had

also been selling everything she had. Now I was really stuck. I walked to Albe Square Mall and

sat in the food court for hours. I remember planning to try and hide while the mall closed and

sleep in those huge flower pots they had near the candy stand in the food court. I left, though,

scared of being locked in there. As I was leaving the mall it started to rain. My new companion,

Murphy's Law, who would become my life long companion, was introducing herself. I mean, it

rained like hell. I went to my original building at 21 St. James Place and sat in the lounging area

where the mailboxes are and tried to dry my legs on the radiator. I watched the rain for a while,

then realized I was hungry as hell. So I went to that candy machine room and looked at those

stale candy bars through the old rusty looking glass for about ten minutes before I decided to go

home.

To my surprise my parents had been quite worried about me. They had recruited help

from one of my childhood hero, Uncle Junior Buck, and he organized a small search party to

look for me. It was about 3:00 a.m. on a school night and I was still only twelve. All I could

think about that night was that my golden goose was gone. But I realized one thing for sure: a

woman who has declared herself a whore will never starve and you will never starve as long as

she considers herself your whore. But when push comes to shove and she is gone, she will still eat because she has pussy to sell while you, my friend, will surely starve.

Things did indeed take a turn for the worse after that, and I would like to thank a few people who got me through such lean times. Wesley Trapp who always brought me something from the store and. Walani Stephens, who not only was the first person on earth to own a microwave; but used it to feed me on countless occasions. And also the entire Horton family, especially Mrs. Peggy Horton, who was like a surrogate mother to me. Mrs. Horton had three sons: Lance, Jeffrey and Glenn, who was one of my best friends. She opened her house up to me and Wesley. I was even allowed there when no one else was home. Believe it or not, the door was always literally open. When she brought home food for her sons, she would bring extra for me. She was passionate about planning one's future and constantly gave me advice. In short, she cared.

Needless to say, my first journey into the world of pimping had ended abruptly.

Chapter Four

"Pimpin' Crack"

From 1984 to 1988; when I was in Port Richmond High School, crack became king. It was really turning the mightiest people into slaves and the world on its ear. Reaganomics was in full swing and money was everywhere. It was a good time to be black and in New York City. Crack was to the average black man what alcohol was to Italians in the Roaring Twenties. It provided endless opportunities.

We moved to Staten Island on my birthday in 1984. Staten Island seemed like a strange and distant land. The people there were very different. The suburbs breed a different kind of person. In Brooklyn, everybody thought about money and nothing else. On Staten Island, everybody just wanted to be cool and in style. I still see it as the birthplace of the rich kids who romanticize about being poor.

On the weekends I stayed at my grandmother's apartment at 333 Lafayette Avenue, two blocks from Cambridge Place. It was still home base for me. All of my friends were there and it was the only place that made sense. My Aunt Teenie got me a job as a dispatcher at Orzan Cab Company on Kosciosko Street between Bedford and Nostrand Avenues. I worked the midnight shift. On my second weekend of work, as I walked pass the Lafayette Garden's Projects, I ran across a halfway shabby looking crack head. Say halfway because she still looked attractive but unkept. She hollered out to me: "Pretty Boy." For me that could have only been one of two

people; Candy or Chocolate. I hadn't seen them in about four years. Sure enough, it was Candy.

As she hugged me and admired how I had grown, I could smell that unmistakable musk of raw

half beaten to death vagina that only comes from the long stretches of whoring on the streets.

"Where you headed, pretty boy?"

"To work, I gotta job now."

"No more newspapers; huh? I hope you still in school."

I told her I worked only on the weekends and that I didn't even live in Brooklyn

anymore. I gazed at her and my old crush was coming back. I remembered her smell, even

though she no longer had it, and how beautiful I though she was. I wanted her on G.P., like

settling an old score, but I couldn't let her know it.

"Pretty boy, I think you're old enough now, if you can still get twenty-five dollars."

I told her I had ten; after all, going from dope fiend to crack head was a pretty big

demotion in those days. She wasn't even worth twenty-five dollars.

"Where we gonna do it?"

"At my job, of course."

"Whatchu do any way?"

I informed her that she would find out when we got there.

As we turned on to Kosciosko from Bedford, she got scared. The block is dark, desolate,

and scary. Orzan Cab Service was a little bit more than mid-block across from a senior citizen

building. The gates were always down after dark, so you really could not tell the place was a car

service. When we got to the building. I stopped and announced, "Here we are."

She looked at me with tears in her eyes and started pleading with me not to kill her and that all I had to do was ask for her money and she would have surrendered it. I started laughing hysterically and knocked on the gate. One of the mechanics pulled it up and motioned me in. I told Candy to stay across the street for a while and went in and hugged my Aunt Teenie and got ready for work.

My Aunt Teenie told me what cars were where and how much each cab would have to charge. She then gave me a kiss and went under the half closed gate and on her way, never noticing Candy across the street.

As soon as my Aunt Teenie was out of sight, I motioned for Candy to come inside and pulled the gates down behind us. Orzan Cab Service was attached to Orzan Bus Service, so we kind of had our own little office over to the side that gave us a little privacy. It was really just a room attached with a small bathroom that looked to me like a radio station might look like had I ever saw one.

I sat down, pulled over an additional chair and told her to sit and give me a minute. I spoke into the radio and received feedback from the drivers, hoping she would be impressed.

"Pretty boy, what happened to you?"

"Whachoo mean?"

"I thought you was gonna pimp and be one of the great ones!"

I was crushed for a minute, then remembered old pimping rules that any young mack worth his salt should never forget. It didn't matter that I was fourteen, in high school and working the midnight shift on weekends to get by. What mattered was that I appeared to be a square. As far as working girls go, a square is a terrible thing to be. He is a man worthy of very little respect, a working chump, a john who is to be treated like a trick; not a john who is being

tricked on. The worse thing I could have done in this situation was to make any attempt at an

excuse for myself working here. The one thing working girls respect in this situation is using

your current situation to run a scam or in some way to embezzle from it or to corrupt it. You can

never say something lame like: "Look I'm just starting out, I'm going to work my way through

high school, then maybe I'll go to college, graduate and hopefully I'll get a job making a little bit

less than you or this job is easy. I get paid for doing nothing. Now let's fuck!"

At the time I thought the best thing for me to do was give her a rundown of what scam I

was trying to run and how I could use her help. I told her that I planned to get a regular pay

check from Orzan's Cab Service and crack from my cousin's "friends" in the Fort Green Projects

and sell it with my partner, Rashawn Bell, on Staten Island during the school week. The more

money I had to buy weight in Fort Green, the better.

I asked her if she was still working the track on 3rd Avenue and Douglas. I wanted to see

if I stood a chance on copping her for myself. She was now on crack, and that gave me the

opportunity to pull her. A working girl on crack doesn't care who she works for or where she

works as long as you direct her and the high comes fast. Women on crack are not as resourceful

or inventive as dope fiend girls. Dope fiends seem to be in slow motion but their minds are

moving at warp speed. A crack head is all speed and no brains, kind of like a speeding car with

no one behind the wheel.

I told Candy that the cab stand would be an excellent place for her to work. I could watch

her back all night. I would always have food and most importantly crack inside the office where

it was warm. The icing on the cake, which came totally by coincidence, I mean by pure stroke of luck, was the fact that one of my best friends at the time was Glenn Horton whose father owned a house three houses away from the cab stand. Glenn told his father that I was working at Orzan's and that I needed a place to crash sometimes during the night. Mr. Horton let me have a room, where, of course, was where Candy would turn tricks.

Candy got a gleam in her eye when I finished and her look of scorn turned to admiration. She hugged me and started kissing me all over my face. "Pretty boy, I thought you had really squared up for a minute." she said. "I thought you was lost."

I had been thinking about that plan for days but decided to use my measly pay check to get myself and Rashawn started in the crack game. I had no idea that whore money would give us our start that our money would come at rocket speed instead of at a snail's pace. Running into Candy that night put everything into high gear. I would get my money from her, get my weight from "Smurf" in Fort Green and go half with Rashawn on Port Richmond Avenue, where he would have his brothers, Chrissy and Shannon, sell the crack. This was chilli pimpin at its finest or some would say "Pimpin' Crack."

But first I had to be sure I could at least cop Candy for a short while to get some "fast" money out of her. I thought the true way was the best way to that. I had to convince her that I could provide her with a place to sleep and turn tricks, not just that I could provide the crack she needed to handle her "Jones" or be able to bail her out of Brooklyn Central Booking and take her to serve her community service. Most importantly, I had to convince her that I would be her man that she could trust me and that I could care for and watch her. I told her how much that baby oil smell meant to me and that I loved her. She seemed to melt in my arms and embrace me as if we were two newlyweds at the altar.

She asked to see the room where she would be staying; I told her that I had some bullshit work that had to be done first. I told her to sit in the corner in one of the offices and rest a bit. She fell asleep, which was good because it was a busy night and I was dispatching cars all over the place.

I woke her up at four a.m., which was lunchtime for me, then had one of the drivers bring us some food. We were both were starving and devoured the food in what felt like seconds. Then we sat in an uncomfortable silence. I could tell that she was self-conscious, especially after hearing me tell her that I had admired her since I was a child. She asked me if there was somewhere where she could shower. She had freshened up as best she could in the cab stand bathroom, but she wanted to be special for me. I told her that I accepted her just the way she was.

I slowly undressed her, and we really had some heart pounding sex. It was hot, black, funky, nasty and greasy. That description might gross some, but that is just the way I like it. I must admit, though, that all the things I said to her that night was not game. I was telling Candy how I really felt. I just thank God that at this time AIDS was reserved for gays and dope fiends. Once again, I was saved by the times.

Chapter Five

"Getting Pimped"

–50–

I met Arlene on line at the Rooftop Roller Rink on 155th Street in Harlem. From time to time, Candy and I would go there to catch shows that headlined artists like Eric B. and Rakim, KRS 1, Marley Marle and the Juice Crew, rap artists of that era who were mega stars to us but unknown to the rest of the world.

While on line, Candy tapped on Arlene's shoulder and asked her if she was alone. Arlene told her that her cousin Nancy was parking the car and was going to catch up with her on the line. I stood silent while Candy worked her magic with the "sister girl just hanging out routine" to warm her up for me to run game on. By the time Nancy got there, Arlene and Candy were like best friends; by the time we got to the entrance, one would think that all four of us had come to the club together.

While in the club, everyone has to stand in the area around the actual rink until 2:00 a.m. That is when they opened the floor up to dancing. Standing in the crowd, you could smell different types of weed; weed mixed with coke which was called "oolas"; weed mixed with crack, the so-called "woolies"; "primos" cigarettes that had the tobacco removed and replaced with cocaine, and of course that unmistakable minty burnt rubber smell of crack.

I, of course, kept crack, coke, diesel and weed on me. At the time these things were as important as having 5, 10, 20 and 50 dollar bills in your pocket today. To make it clear, those drugs was the currency of the day.

Candy offered Arlene and Nancy some weed; it's important not to scare young girls away with coming out of the sky blue with "Y'all want some crack" kind of talk? "Weed" is more of an ice breaker; it gets people to open up and socialize with each other.

We stood there in our own little cloud of smoke. I made sure I was a part of the conversation, but I did not say too much. Even if you plan to be the star, it is best to always let your girl get the stage for you. If it were up to me, I would not have said anything. I only spoke as much as I did to keep those around us at bay and to give the appearance that this party of three belonged to me.

Candy, with that natural woman's "Gaydar," picked up something in Nancy, and before you knew it, they were sniffing coke and kissing in a dark corner right next to me and Arlene. Boy, Candy was a genius! This gave Arlene the impression that Candy and I were just friends hanging out at the Rooftop and that I was fair game. I did not use drugs or drink, but I was a social dealer. I offered Arlene some coke, but she declined. That turned me on. She was different just like me. As far as I knew, we were the only teenagers in New York that did not sniff "Blow."

My song at the time was "Paid in Full" by Eric B. and Rakim. It came on as they opened up the rink to everyone. Arlene grabbed my hand and led me on to the floor. We danced for a while. She was a very pretty girl. I usually did not favor light skin girls much, but she was different. She was light skinned, but she was built like a dark skinned woman. She also had rich full features like a darker woman. The best way I could describe her was to think of "Florence Griffen Joyner," (Flo-Jo) the Olympic athlete of the day. I stayed quite a while. We danced and talked. I let her take the lead in the conversation, but I could not tell whether she was a square or not. I mean, I could tell for sure if she was a working girl, but knew she was not a street girl or a good girl. She did not seem like a stranger to drugs or to those who used drugs. She also carried herself like someone who expected to be respected.

I began to feel a very strong attraction to Arlene. It was not as if I wanted to have sex with her. It was as if I wanted to be with her and for her to belong to me. After about two hours

of telling our life stories to each other, doing the 'wop", the "baseball bat", and the "Pee Wee

Herman", we realized that we had not seen Candy and Nancy since we saw them kissing. We

looked all over the club for them but they were nowhere to be found. We stepped outside and

still nothing. We looked in Rucker Park across the street, and still nothing.

Arlene said, "Let me check the car." As we approached the car from the front, we could

see that the passenger front seat had been laid all the way down and Candy had laid Nancy on

her back, slid up to the top of the seat and was eating her out. Arlene laughed and told me that

her cousin was crazy. She asked me to walk her to the store on 8th Avenue, the one next to

"Mamas Fried Chicken." I told her that the place was not safe, especially for people like us out-

of-towners. She told me to relax; she knew everybody.

She was not lying. Once we were on 8th Avenue, she was greeted by everyone. She

laughed and kissed and looked very comfortable; I started to relax. People in New York have a

way of making you feel invisible.

After buying a soda and some chips, she wanted to sit and talk in Rucker's Park. As we

crossed the street, about fifty motorcycles came roaring up 8th Avenue, doing wheelies and all

kind of tricks. The guy leading the pack pulled over and the rest of them followed him. She

kissed me on the cheek and instructed me to wait for her in the park. The guy on the motorcycle

seemed curious as to who I was. I made sure not to make eye contact too long with him or

anyone with him. These dudes looked dangerous.

I waited on the corner directly across from Mamas Fried Chicken, but I stood there

looking as if I was making sure Arlene was alright. I could tell the dude Arlene was talking to thought it was funny.

After they finished talking, he kissed her on the cheek and then told her loud enough for me to hear, "Make sure that little nigger don't leave that bottle in the park." He then took off on one wheel with his whole crew behind him, making so much noise that I could not hear myself think. Even when they were in front of the club, I had to scream to Arlene for her to hear me.

"Who was that dude?"

"Oh, that's my cousin Alberto," Arlene said.

"What did you call him though?"

"I called him 'PO', You never heard of him?"

"No," I said cluelessly.

"Everybody knows him as "Alpo," He's very important here."

I definitely saw opportunity here. As we sat and talked on the bleachers in the park, I felt like I was on a tropical island, not across the street from a club, where men were waving cars at three in the morning and pit bulls were tied to the fence. While we were talking, she asked me what I really needed versus what I really wanted. I told her that I was not sure whether I wanted to pimp or to deal drugs. Times were changing.

When I was 10, pimps were the most powerful men around and everything a black man could aspire to be. Now in 1985, drug dealers were on top. I know at this point that pimping Arlene was out of the question, but if I were to become her boyfriend, then maybe I could reach the promise land. Besides, I was young and stupid, meaning I really wanted to be her boyfriend. "You know, I got a little money," if I cold get some weight for a good price, I could really make some money."

She said shyly, "You mean from my cousin?"

I replied shyly, "No, from you. Besides, he wouldn't trust dealing with me; he's too important."

"How much you got to spend?" she said curiously.

"About $500 dollars."

She stared at me, then burst into laughter. She laughed so hard, she started crying.

"Five Hundred Dollars? Nigger, this is Harlem! You made it sound like you was a big timer or something."

I stood there quietly. I sure had felt as if I was, but that was by Brooklyn standards. Just having a car, any car makes you a somebody in Brooklyn. But you can't even call yourself a man in Harlem without one.

She made me feel better about myself by telling me how cute she thought I was. I remember thinking that there was no way I could let Candy hear her talk to me like this. Candy would surely completely lose respect for me. She said confidently: "Walk me over to the phone."

At the phone she beeped someone and did not wait for an answer, but just said, "Let's go back to the club." Since the Rooftop stamped your hand, you could go in and out at your leisure. She positioned me up against the wall and backed up against me, placing my arms around her. She leaned back and whispered in my ear. "How much did you think you were going to get for five hundred?" I knew that coke went for about $15 a gram in Brooklyn, so 35 grams would cost about $525.00, which, in turn, would have to be cooked to make crack. That's how you really made your money.

I told her about 35 grams. "By the way, how do you know what I want?" I said with a slick smile.

"Oh I know, believe me, I know," Arlene said.

Right about then, a short dark skinned girl walked up to us and placed a brown paper bag in Arlene's hand. Arlene said, "Let's go find my crazy cousin."

Back at Arlene's car, Candy and Nancy were just sitting in the car, listening to music. Arlene embraced me in front of them and kissed me passionately, as if she wanted to see Candy's response. It turned not to be a smile. Candy got out of the car and embarrassed me by also kissing me, just not as passionately. Her kiss was very wet, sticky and smelled really good, if you know what I mean. Then she asked me: "Daddy, they gonna drive us to the train station?" I looked at Arlene with a questioning expression.

Arlene replied, "I can't, not as dirty as you are."

I wondered, how in the hell does she know about the drugs I have on me! She then tossed me the brown paper bag, in a way that was sure to get Candy' attention. I didn't even check it; I just pulled her aside to thank her. "I don't owe you anything?"

"No Mick-man," Arlene said.

"You sure?" I replied.

"If you want more, call me. If you want more than that pay me a visit. I live out in Hempstead, Long Island."

She then handed me a piece of paper with all of her info on it. I kissed her again and gave Nancy a kiss on the cheek. Candy gave Nancy a big wet kiss and grabbed her butt as she did it, then smiled, winked and said "mmh-h". Candy and I made our way expeditiously up 155th Street to the staircase that would take us from Sugar Hill to the train station at St. Nicholas Avenue and the A train back to Brooklyn. Candy went to sleep in Glenn's father's house while I went to my

grandmother's. I then checked the bag in the bathroom. There was a lot of shit in this bag. It was

hard and beige. I thought: "What the hell is this?" I had thought that Arlene was going to give me

powdered coke. I took a tiny bit out and brought it to my cousin, Cliffy, who also stayed with my

grandmother, so that he could tell me what it was.

"It's crack! Cliffy said. What the hell do you think it is?"

I didn't know that you could buy ready made crack. At this time most of the people still

did not. I weighed it on a friend's triple beam and it came out to 250 grams. It was one-eighth of

a kilo and free.

I was getting no sleep on the weekends. I was dispatching cabs and working the hell out

of Candy all night. Then I would lay up with Arlene all day. I was exhausted. I had tried

numerous times to score for free with Arlene, but it was in vein. She knew I was hooked on her

both as a connection and sexually. There was no way I could get crack anywhere else at the price

I was getting it for from her and she knew it.

I would leave her house on Sunday afternoon and ride the Long Island Railroad to

Flatbush Ave to the same stop where I sold newspapers as a child. Then I would take the double

"R" to 95th Street to catch the S57 to Castleton Ave on Staten Island. Once I reached my

neighborhood, I would head to Harrison Avenue where an up and coming young man, a few

years younger than myself, who had help me brainstorm this whole idea in the first place, was

waiting for the product. The connection, Rashawn Bell, along with his brother Chrissy and

Shannon, were some of the wildest young boys ever. Although Chrissy didn't hustle with us, I

could always call on Rashawn to do bodily harm to someone, even if it was just for fun. Shannon was the best "hustler." He would put in long hours grinding on Port Richmond Avenue. A crack

sale was like a high to him and he could not stop making sales. He used his mother's medicine

bottles to carry vials of crack. It is a method a lot of people in that neighborhood use to this day.

During the week, usually around Wednesday, any drugs that I had brought from Long

Island would usually be tapped out. Rashawn said that we could buy all the crack we wanted in

Harlem; all we had to do was get there. He told me that in the 140's Dominicans would offer you

whatever you wanted, even offering to cook it for you to your specifications.

That very night I stole my parent's brand new van. My friends were very impressed as we

drove slowly to the destination. We were totally silent knowing damn well that if we were caught

this night, we might be gone for years. As I got off at the 155th Street exit off of the FDR,

everyone seemed to tense up. This was the land of legends after all. I knew that the road up to the

top of 155th Street took you to Sugar Hill, but I did not know how to get on it. I accidently drove

all the way up 155th to Bradhurst. At that time, you could only make a left, which I did to 145th. I

made a right and I was there on Sugar Hill, the last place left on earth that could make a black

man's dreams come true. We made a left onto Broadway, then a U-turn at 139th Street to survey

the whole of the 140's to see all the Dominicans we had heard of. We were not disappointed.

They were everywhere selling drugs a mile a minute. We pulled over at 141st and just sat for a

second.

"Well, whose gonna go get the shit?" I said. "I drove all the way up here that's my

contribution." Rashawn knew I was talking to him, and we all knew he was the perfect candidate

for the job. He seemed to be destined for greatness. This scene felt like he was crossing over to

manhood. I felt happy to help him along the trail to being the biggest drug dealer in our neighborhood. Rashawn got out of the van looking real serious with a face of stone. He was back in minutes. He jumped in the van screaming, "They robbed me, let's get the fuck out of here!" He then pulled the curtain back screaming, "What motherfucker! What!" I was pulling at top speed before he started laughing and told me to calm down, that everything was fine. He even said the dealer threw in five extra grams for buying so much and that we should ask for Jose from now on.

Now it was my turn to do the hardest part of the deal we did that night, and that was to get us home unmolested by the police.

"You think you can do it?" Rashawn asked.

"Yeah," I said. "I'm fifteen now. I can drive pretty good." I took Riverside Drive knowing that sooner or later I would see an entrance to the West Side Highway. All the while when I saw cops, I would freeze. Everyone would start screaming to scare me. Then they would tell me to relax, that I was doing fine. When we got home I got a firm handshake and hug from all of them. I felt like the captain who safely delivered his passengers after flying through a hurricane. It was a great accomplishment, especially for a boy who could not drive worth shit. As they were cutting up the drugs, I went filled up the gas to half full, exactly where it was before we left, parked in my mother's driveway and knocked on my sister Shana's window to let me in.

After I returned from school the next afternoon, Rashawn rang my bell. He handed me my share and told me that they were almost tapped out already. Until I figured out a way to get them weight during the week, it was hard to keep telling them "no" all the time. I could only take them on Wednesday or Thursday, or I could bring them weight on Sunday night.

Boy, the money rolled in. I was having so much fun with Candy while I worked. I even got jealous a few times when she had to turn tricks. My shift began at midnight, so a few times

Candy and I went out before my shift started and would go to the "Deuce" or, as some people

called it, 42nd Street. We danced and had fun in clubs like Latin Quarters, the Rooftop, and

Union Square. Candy even took me to The View, a revolving spinning restaurant on top of the

Marriott Hotel. She took me shopping too, measuring me for clothes and even turning me on to

new foods I had never tried, such as raw clams, one of my favorites to this day.

As a result of all this personal growth, my grades once again suffered. I hadn't learned at

this point to simply bribe teachers into passing me as I would later on in high school. So like

your typical dumb nigger I bucked the system. I landed in summer school as a result. But to my

surprise it was fun. I had an eighteen-year old girl named, Lisa Rivera in my class. Her mother

was white and they lived like white people. She lived within walking distance to New Dorp High

School. There was just the two of them, but as you know white people live very differently than

black or latino people. They lived like care free beach bum druggies right off of the beach. I

mean this girl did not care about anything. One day while walking down the beach, I complained

that my shoes were getting dirty by the sand. She kicked even more sand on my new kicks. Then

right out in the open she pulled her shorts off and ran bottomless under the boardwalk, where we

made love madly. She whispered in my ear, "Don't worry about bullshit like dirty sneakers when

you got a bad girl like me on top of all that money you getting off the street."

I lifted my head and looked deep into her hazel eyes. I had not told her I was dealing

drugs, but I was sure wearing the uniform of a drug dealer: a big gold chain, brand new sneakers

and the name clothes of the day: Street and Chic, Christian Dior, Ralph Lauren, Le Cog Sportif,

Izod, etc. I guess it did not take a genius to figure it out. She smiled, winked and whispered

"Hustler". We continued like dogs in heat. What a great summer that was!

This went on for a couple of years; everything was going like clockwork. I even looked forward to summer school. To keep my parents at bay, I took a janitor's job at the C.Y.O. (The Catholic Youth Organization) on Anderson Avenue. It gave me extra money and a safe place to meet with Rashawn and the crew. After a couple of years, they were all full fledged gangster. I mean, no half-stepping, they were full blown. We all owed it to Candy and Arlene; they were the source of all our happiness and wealth. By this time, though, Rashawn really did not need me anymore. I was putting out less and less and got back less and less. It had been over two years that this little sweet relatively unknown hustle had been going on. We knew it couldn't last forever, but the end was swift and devastating; I let that experience with Lisa River fool me.

White people like Lisa and her mother do not have the same worries we do. No matter how much money we make, we must always be prepared for our unceremonious return to the gutter. I am sometimes torn in my thoughts about this issue. I sometimes wish I would have slapped that girl that day at the beach and said, "fuck you girl, my sneakers cost 100 dollars." Sometimes I remember us under the boardwalk as a highlight in my life. I guess I learned from Lisa to open up and have fun. I learned from up coming events to have fun wisely and never loose focus.

I was having so much damn fun I had not even noticed how terrible she looked. As I bend over to get my shot for gonorrhea, syphilis and chlamydia, I can honestly say I had no idea where I caught them. I was as promiscuous as I could be, even though I was just seventeen at this point, I was well aware that times were changing. I had lost four cousins to AIDS at this point and could feel change in the air.

Candy and I were in Glenn's father's house on Kosciosko Street when I pulled out a

condom. She laughed at me wickedly and said, "Don't let that money go to your head, silly little

nigger!" She thought that my wanting to use a condom meant I thought I was better than her, that

I thought she was dirty, that I thought I could get her money and escape the dirt that came along

with it. You know what? She was absolutely RIGHT. But I could not tell her that I had not

developed the art of "Coothe" at this point. I simply tried to explain that I was embarrassed by

being at the doctor's office using my mothers HIP Card and didn't want to be embarrassed again.

"I thought you was a pimp using your mother's card like some mama's boy?" Candy said

sarcastically. I gotta admit it did sound corny. Needless to say, I knew I would blow her

eventually. I knew I would. It was the beginning of the end but I tried to fight it like niggers

always do. At the C.Y.O. I felt humiliated; I would see Rashawn and his brothers riding around

in a brand new Lexus at the ripe age of fifteen while I worked like a clown. They had people

working for them who were ten years older.

I would say, what's up Rashawn. Y'all niggers getting rich, huh? He would say, "You

can too Mick. You know the deal. It's little risk, little reward."

I felt the walls closing in for sure. I figured I still had Candy, even though I knew it

would not be for long. I also had Arlene as a connect but without Rashawn selling the well oiled

machine I had created, it would come to a grinding halt. I had told Candy that I had Arlene

working a track out on Long Island, but I do not think she believed me. Still, Candy seemed to

care more about me, while Arlene just wanted to screw me. I also felt very inferior to Long

Island people, they seemed much more worldly and sophisticated than I was. In short, I felt out

classed.

Arlene came by my school in the middle of the week and beeped me. She invited me to a party that night. I stole my parents van the same way I did for the uptown runs and went to Long Island.

At the party, Arlene told me she had a friend there who saw my picture that Arlene had on her dresser and who was dying to have sex with me. "I wouldn't mind at all if you did it," Arlene said. "But only once." I took a look at the girl and thought she was good looking, I was feeling down at how bleak my future was looking, so I said, "What the hell" and went into the back room and had sex with the girl. I enjoyed it immensely. Two hours later Arlene came to me again with another friend, also good looking, I had sex with her also.

At the end of the party I approached Arlene for some crack, fully prepared to pay full price and was pleasantly surprised with an "eighth" for free. I went home with a smile, thinking about the good time I had had and the prospect of the quick turnover from Rashawn.

Money had been tight for a while, so getting it was a breath of fresh air. For the next few weeks, the parties became routine. Let me just say one thing about a young man at seventeen being introduced to a lot of pretty women to have sex with. In no way did I feel like I was being used. I thought I was getting over like a fat rat. I thought that Arlene was a liberal soul who was just sharing me with her friends. I also thought that Arlene was giving the drugs to me for free because she loved me as she claimed she did all the time. I was very impressed with Arlene. She seemed to know everything, she also seemed to know all the right people.

We always had to feel fortunate and grateful just to know somebody who knew a real somebody. Arlene was the first real case of this. She seemed to know everyone who was somebody today and that included many rappers and gangsters.

I went to a party at Arlene's in the Spring of 1987. I was excited Arlene had told me the night before about how beautiful the girls who were going to be at this particular party. And boy were they. Not only were the women she hooked me up with beautiful, they were also grown mature women. I was also excited at the thought of money I could get if I could convince Arlene to break me off some "free" crack.

While in the middle of having sex in the back room, I heard shots ring out! Everybody ran from the apartment and down one flight of stairs to Terrace Avenue. Everybody, that is except Arlene, Nancy, Arlene's brother, Sly and I. Sly closed the door and all of us stood there, looking down at the dead man on the living room floor. I ran into the room to put my clothes on. When I came back out I interrupted Arlene arguing with the girl I was having sex with.

"I paid you Arlene!" the girl said.

"I ain't get my money's worth," Arlene snapped.

"Bitch, you see what's going on, Get the fuck out of here!"

Arlene screamed; she was pissed off.

I could not believe it, I had been getting pimped all this time and did not know it. Women had actually being paying to have sex with me. I was appalled and flattered at the same time. This had only happened because I thought so little of myself. I did not even think that I was worth the crack I was begging for after being pimped. I felt so dirty and used that it embarrasses me to this day.

"Bitch, bitches been paying you to fuck me," I yelled at Arlene. "Where the fuck is my money?"

Sly said, "Mick-man slow down, you were having fun, weren't you?"

Sly grabbed the woman who had tricked me by her arm, dragged her to the door way and threw her down the stairs.

"Mick-man get dressed. We gotta get rid of this body," Arlene ordered.

"Nigger, I ain't helping you with shit! I said that ain't my problem."

I went into a room to get dressed. Arlene, Sly and Nancy came into the room behind me. I turned and noticed that Sly had a gun in his hand. "We got a problem little nigger. Either you help us with this body or we gonna be getting rid of two bodies, his and your little yellow ass," Sly warned.

"Alright, alright, I'll do it," I said. I sat down on the edge of the king size brass bed and slipped on my sneakers. I told them that I would be right out. I had to get my things from out of Arlene's room because after this I was through with her ass. Arlene interrupted us with a loud laugh.

"You clown, you are so arrogant, you didn't even realize at the roof-top the night we met that I was a pimp and Nancy was my ho who preoccupied your bitch so I could get in your head. You think you got game! You's a lame chump! We been pimpin' your ass for months and making a killing too. On top of it all, your bitch in Brooklyn knows it too. You would have blown her by now if she wasn't such a junkie, crackhead. We are through chump!"

I said to Arlene, "I know what. Keep this shit you brought me. Let's get this over with so I can be on my way".

We all walked out to the living room and there we saw the dead body. He was about 19 years old or so. He looked about 6'1", medium complexion with a high-top fade. He was wearing a Guess sweatshirt under a Guess jean suit, Spot Built blue and white sneakers, and a thick rope gold chain. His mouth hung open. I could see that his two front teeth were gold

capped. Sly took all the gold down to his teeth. He then instructed me to follow him into the

bedroom to get blankets to wrap him in. While in the room, Arlene called Sly to the living room

for something. I stood there waiting for him and suddenly I felt very threatened, as if my life was

in imminent danger. I went for the window, which had a fire escape that lead to the back alley.

When I got down, I heard Sly scream out the window, "That's your ass, nigger."

The gun shoots sounded like booming thunder, I just kept going. If that gun only had

sixteen shots, then I must have heard echoes because it sounded like a thousand shots. I hit the

ground, went to Terrace Avenue and made a left. If I had run into Arlene I would surely be ghost

right now. I knew she had an Uzi. I cut down the back of the project building to Atlantic Avenue.

Instead of running toward the bus terminal, I ran toward Garden City. Anyone reading this book

familiar with this area knows that a nigger would have to be crazy to go there. I ran to a safe

looking bus stop along the N6 route and rode it to Hillside Avenue, where I picked up the double

"R" train. All I could think of was that I had lost my connect. In the world I knew then, it was a

God damned catastrophe.

When drugs are your business, loosing your connect is about the worst thing that can

happen to you. I went home empty handed that weekend. I mean I had money from Candy and

my measly ass pay but no crack shit. It was the crack that made me somebody in Port Richmond.

Now it was gone. I told Rashawn that we could try on Wednesday. He agreed, but we both knew

I was just about out of the game. At least I still had Candy. I decided I would focus on her and

maybe clean her up a little. I even started to imagine a future with her. What can I say? I was

only seventeen! She made me happy and my life worth living. Now my weekends were great;

my week days, were terrible. I would slave at the C.Y.O. while Rashawn was living like a king. I would wait for Candy to call when I came to Brooklyn in the middle of the week. That call never came.

I waited week after week. Still the call never came. I was devastated. I quit the taxi stand job and began to just hang around my friend Glenn's house. Although Wes was finding himself more and more busy at Pathmark, he was still a regular there also.

The only money I had coming in was my janitorial check from the C.Y.O. ... pathetic! Glenn was doing just as bad; he worked at Roy Rogers in Times Square. We were like children, the way both of us found ourselves depending on Wes. He paid our way into the clubs or movies, and when he bought his brand new Mercury Cougar, he even drove us to our girlfriends' houses. This was a real low point in my life.

In Staten Island, Rashawn, Chrissy and Shannon were riding high, too "high". Chrissy died in an auto accident. Rashawn seemed to constantly be at war after this. It went on for about 12 years to be exact. The constant ambushes and the shooting up of his mother's house weakened Rashawn. People in the neighborhood sensed this; they told Rashawn, Shannon and their people to stay off of Port Richmond Avenue. It was now theirs. They could only sell on Harrison Avenue, the people said.

Rashawn and Shannon refused to comply. One of their workers knocked on my door one night and told me that Shannon had just gotten killed and was at that moment lying on Port Richmond Avenue. I walked to the scene and took a look. Shannon had been blown open something terrible. He was hit three times with a .44 Magnum. He had holes in him that appeared to be the size of tennis balls. Of all the hustlers I knew Shannon is recognized as among the best.

He was the care type of hustler. Even though he was fifteen, Shannon was all business. To the best of my knowledge, he did not drink or smoke. Shannon never carried on in the street, most and to hand street dealers are really hanging out as they hustle. Not Shannon: one time as a party was going on at the bell house, Shannon walked past us freshly showered on his way to Port Richmond Avenue for a long night of non-stop hand to hand drug dealing. I admired his work ethic. Rest in Peace Shannon.

I saw a cop removing medicine bottles from his jacket. For years to come I would keep crack vials in medicine bottles just like I saw Shannon do. Police have overlooked them time and time again, and later as a narcotics officer, I made numerous arrests by finding other people's stashes in medicine bottles. If I did not arrest them, I kept the drugs for re-sale.

With Chrissy and Shannon dead, that left Rashawn feeling seriously vulnerable. It's a good thing he was not alone. Rashawn had a lot of young boys working for him who really admired him. But none were as true to the game as Chrissy and Shannon. He was snitched on repeatedly until he found himself in prison. Years later when Rashawn came home from jail I was in my third year as a police officer. I gave Rashawn three thousand dollars to get some crack to get back in the game.

He knocked on my door three days after and handed me six thousand dollars. Soon I heard everywhere that Rashawn was back and getting rich on the street. It felt good to help my old friend. Weeks later, he too died in an auto accident. All the rest of his crew became crack heads. None of them are worth mentioning by name.

With Rashawn, Chrissy, Shannon, Arlene and Candy gone, my crack pimping high school days came to an end.

After bribing a teacher, I was able to graduate. Needless to say, I got more of an education on the street than I did school, courtesy of the realest niggers I ever knew.

Chapter Six

"Jail Pimpin"

Two years after graduating from high school, I was sworn in as a NYC Correction Officer. At this point there were three jails and one mental ward that exclusively housed women and I worked in all four of them. As a result, I really got to know women, especially from a criminal view point. At first I just did my job and did not interact with the female inmates at all. I basically acted as if I worked at a cattle ranch and was responsible for her. Keeping my distance angered them and that anger grew to fury. It resulted in me being sexually assaulted twice by female inmates. Each time, all parties involved were given ninety days a piece in the "bing," which is solitary confinement. They all told me later that it was worth every minute.

I started to feel frustrated trying to control these women when it dawned on me: "When have women ever been controlled by the book?" Maybe the Salem Witch Trials that is about it. The event changed my attitude it was a big fight that lead to the "Cecit" or riot squad to be called.

I was working at Wards Island Correctional Facility for sentenced women. There was an A and a B officer for a dorm that housed one hundred and twenty women. The A officer kept the count and did all administrative work. The B officer took the count, made a tour of the area every fifteen minutes and was really held responsible for the care, custody and control of the inmates. I hated making a tour of the dorm because that is when you saw all the shit you really did not want to see, especially since it was your job to stop them from robbing, raping and abusing each other. I would try my best to make them aware that I was walking through the cubes, corridors and my least favorite place, the bathroom, so that nothing inappropriate would be going on. But of course, they made sure I always walked in on them right on time to see the middle of the act. They seemed to love to do that to me. On this particular day, about fifty screaming inmates came running at me and another officer, telling us that there was a big fight going on in the bathroom. A girl was getting jumped and stabbed; she might die (I could have waited for the "Goon Squad"). The girl was Norma Jean Williams, who was friendly toward me, so I didn't mind trying to help her, but being the B officer, I had to do something. I decided to try and save her.

I saw three inmates in the bathroom in the middle of beating, stripping Norma Jean of her clothes. I charged them, screaming, "LET HER GO!" I began pulling them apart and barking out orders to cease this nonsense. Water and soap was flying everywhere. All of a sudden, I saw the hats and bats of the goon squad as they stormed into the bathroom. The girls froze and so did I. I heard a few of my fellow officers begin to laugh from under their riot helmets. All of the girls were almost completely naked. My pants were pulled down to my ankles. The scene looked ridiculous. I was looked all around. I tried to focus, wiping away the water and soap in my hair and eyes. Suddenly, I noticed that she was down on her knees and had put my penis into her mouth right in front of the squad.

Of course, I was called into the captain's office to explain just what the hell was going on. I told them exactly what happened, but he still found it hard to believe. "I'm going to let this slide since your mother's my boss," Captain Perez said. For that I was most grateful. My mother retired ten years later as a warden of H.D.M., the house of detention for men on Riker's Island.

The next day I strongly considered resigning from the Corrections Department. Even though I did not, the seed was planted in my mind. A year later I did resign to be sworn in as a New York City police officer. The aspect of work I feared the most was chow time. I had to supervise the "blind-feeding" of the inmates, which meant I stood by a slot, knocked and put the tray in for next inmate in line. I had to stand up front in front of five hundred female inmates who had all seen my penis the day before, as well as several dozen correction officers. I have worked with male and female inmates, and when it comes to giving officers hell, the females are far worse. Those girls were shouting all kinds of obscenities at me from every corner of the chow hall. Norma Jean Williams was not charged or written up for anything. After all, she was the so-called victim who I was trying to rescue. Finally, it was her turn to come to the window for her tray. The whole chow hall fell silent to see how we dealt with one another. I just stood there and did my best not to make eye contact, Norma Jean leaned toward me and said, "Take it easy, Officer Gourdine. At least it isn't small." I smiled and just nodded.

About a month later, I applied to have a "steady" dorm on the three to eleven tour. At the time my mother was a deputy warden at the Rose M. Singer Correctional Facility on Riker's Island. So I was a shoe in to get the post.

I would be working alone on the third floor with only seventy-five females. I kept the keys so no one could get on or off my floor unless I said so. My power was absolute, but I was a very kind lord and my "ladies" appreciated it. After about two weeks of blowing off steam, being an asshole and telling everyone how my house was going to be run, I settled into a groove.

One day while making a tour of my area, an inmate named "Quickness," whose legal name was Janice Quick and to whom I professionally referred to as Ms. Quick, invited me to play a game of Scrabble with her and her woman. Ms. Quick was about twenty five years older

than me. Her woman was about my age. I was looking forward to playing a game I had never

played before. I did not realize that Ms. Quick was using me as eye candy for her woman.

The next week after my pass days, Ms. Quick told me, as I entered the dorm, that her

woman could not leave the bunk because she was being punished for fantasizing about me too

much. I was just supposed to turn her on, but she was becoming obsessed with me. Ms. Quick

told me that she valued my company and appreciated the little favors that I had done for her and

her woman, especially serving as their Scrabble partner. Ms. Quick offered her woman to me for

a taste. She claimed it was a friendly gesture. I respectfully declined, of course, thanked her,

patted her on the shoulder and challenged her to a game of Scrabble.

Let me set the reader straight by saying one thing right now. Only a woman can teach you

the pimp game. A man can give you advice and steer you in the right direction, but nobody

knows women like a woman. I sincerely believe that. Ms. Quick took me to school.

As the days passed and after her woman got off of punishment, we went from playing

Scrabble to bringing in other players. Some played spades and shot dice, all the while getting a

top notch education in game.

I had not realized for at least three months that a full fledge prostitution ring was being

run in my dorm. In fact, it was being run from our gambling table in the middle of the day

room. Yes sir, Ms. Quick got so comfortable with me that she would talk about her business right

in front of me. We would sit there playing cards when a young girl would run up to her and kiss

her on the lips. Ms. Quick would say "T.T." give me a box of squares at "rec." Make sure you go

to her "bunk" after lights out. As Ms. Quick spoke to her, the young girl winked at me and said,

"Too bad you don't work midnights, 'cause we could really have some fun. " I just sat stone faced, never wanting to reveal just how turned on I was by the whole scene.

Sometime later that week, when Ms. Quick and I were playing "War", I asked her about her pimping, but who can be pimped, who should be pimped, who makes the best hoe, how do you run girls on the street. I picking her brain. Deep down I wanted the same control she had. Up until this point, even with Candy, I had been winging it. I had watched pimping growing up, and while dealing with Candy I was playing it by ear. Even though I knew about the game I listened to Ms. Quick with the attentiveness of a kindergartner. To my surprise, Candy had been ripping my ass off and so had Nobi Jones. When I told Ms. Quick that, she laughed and said, "Those bitches don't really know the game either. Furthermore, they weren't trying to get money; they were trying to get high, and believe it or not, you weren't controlling them. They were controlling you. You weren't pimping, you were simping."

Ms. Quick told me not to take it personally. That was just how women work. A woman will keep you asleep to the point that you will get the short end of the stick for as long as she can could do it, all the while making you feel like a king. She then told me that she was going to let me in on a little secret. "I'm really running the third floor, not you," she explained. I even made you my friend when you became our steady officer to make myself even more powerful."

She went even further to prove her point. She called two girls over and told them to sweep and mop the dorm, even though they were not my house gang. She said, "the house gang includes my girls and the pay they get they give to me. So you see, Officer Gourdine I'm the real C.O. and the pimp of this house. All I had to do was make you believe that we were friends." I thought about everything she had taught me over the past few months, especially the pimp

Lingo.

I said, "Ms. Quick! You're wrong. You are not the real C.O. of this floor or the pimp, for that matter. I think you've taught me better than that. You taught me that what you are is my "bottom bitch." Don't you forget it. If you do, I'll pack your ass up and send you to the Island. Do I make myself clear, Ms. Quick?" She smiled at me sheepishly and replied, "Yes Daddy". She then looked around to see if there were be any witnesses. She made sure no one saw her act in a feminine way. Then she batted her eyes at me, spun on her heels and walked away for a few feet. She returned to her regular strut when she though someone could be watching.

Ms. Quick and I grew close as time went by. She gave me a calm, smooth self-running house, and I gave her permission to run her stable. We became not only Scrabble partners, but also confidants. I even stood in full uniform as "best man" at her wedding in the Wards Island Prison yard. I made sure through my connections, of course, that she and her "wife" had a honeymoon at night alone in the yard. I really enjoyed that show. The next day, I brought in chips, pretzels and koolaid and let them decorate their cubicle with toilet paper so we could have a proper reception.

Wards Island Correction Institute for women closed six months later. Ms. Quick was transferred to the Rose M. Singer Center on Riker's Island to serve the rest of her sentence. I hugged her as she got on the bus and thanked her for teaching me the game properly. She said, "The game ain't to be told; the game is to be sold and you paid for it." I said, "How'd you figure it?" She smiled and said, "I made a ton of money in here while you were in charge, but nothing is going to compare to what you're gonna make with everything I taught you." She winked at me and said, "Now go get'em, pimp." She got on the bus and rode out of my life.

Chapter Seven

"Police Officer Pimp"

After two and a half years of being a correction's officer my number was called at the

New York City Police Department (NYPD). I had taken the test at the age of sixteen and after

six- and-a-half years, I was about to join New York City's finest. I felt lucky, I heard rumors that

people have waited as long as ten years to be sworn in as a New York City police officer.

After being thoroughly brainwashed at the Police Academy for six months, I was

assigned to the 67th Precinct at 2820 Snyder Avenue in East Flatbush Brooklyn, New York. I was

ready to do some serious crime fighting; I mean I was really pumped up. We were first put into

"F.T.U." units, or field training units. Each unit included four probationary police officers, or

rookies, and one senior officer, our training officer.

On my very first day, we in the unit witnessed a drug buy. My fellow officers were

amazed by my incredible sixth sense. "How in the world did you know they were making a drug

transaction?" Officer Malta said. I spotted it before anyone else did. I chased the dealer and

tackled him to the ground. It was my best Hollywood style arrest, one that I had envisioned in

my head a million times in the last six months at the Academy.

"Just a cop's hunch, I guess." I replied, trying not to let on that I, myself, had made the

same transaction hundreds, if not thousands, of times.

I brought my captured prey to the sergeant's desk so that the dealer could be properly

charged. I love to be credited with my first arrest. My chest stuck way out as I walked in front of

the desk saying loudly as they patted on my back, "You broke your cherry, kid.

Congratulations!" I was actually the first rookie in my class to make an arrest. The desk officer

said, "I have to go find the Desk Sergeant."

I just stood there and stood there and stood there. Finally Sgt. Roundtree appeared. To my

utter shock, he was black. Up until that point, I do not think I had ever seen one before. A brother like me, I thought. He's going to be so happy that I am making us look good. He might even make me his Assistant Desk Officer!!!"

"What is this shit!" Sgt. Roundtree said, looking at the three crack vials that I had neatly stood side by side on his desks. "That's the evidence sir," I explained. I witnessed the whole transaction and made the arrest."

"You woke me up for three fucking crack vials?" "You fucking idiot." The whole precinct erupted in laughter. The perp that I had arrested began to laugh, too. Then whole precinct fell silent.

"Shut the FUCK UP!!" Sergeant Roundtree growled at the perp.

After a few moments of deafening silence, Sgt. Roundtree instructed me to cut him loose. I said, "What about the crack, sir?"

"Give it back to him, if you want! Sergeant said. I don't care if you smoke it! Just don't wake me up for bullshit again!"

I walked the perp down the Perp Walk and out the back door. I took the cuffs off of him, explaining that I was new and did not know any better.

"What about my crack?" he said. He sounded as though he were trying to intimidate me in front of my fellow officers. I told him that the crack was mine, so get lost. If he had asked me nicely, I might have given the crack back to him.

Criminal contacts usually find you when you're a police officer. What really disappoints is when you extend a favor to a career criminal, hoping that you have proven yourself and hoping that the criminal will let you be a part of their ongoing criminal enterprise. But they really do not know or trust you well enough to let you in.

Such was the case with Riccardo Smith, or "Inch," which was his name on the street. Riccardo had been with my cousin, Shamina, who I have called Mina since I was fifteen. He was smooth and the very definition of hustler. He was always well dressed, always well mannered, and well spoken and drove a mean car that had the sweet smell of dirty money. He had given me a few rides to the train station as a teenager. He would ask me what I planned to do with myself. I would say, "I just want some money, man" and he would say, while pulling huge rolls of money out of all his pockets "Oh, you mean like this!" He loved making me foam from the mouth. Yup! He was someone I wanted to be down with.

One day, while walking the beat on Nostrand Avenue near the Vanderveer Houses, I got raised on my radio and told to come to the station house. When I got there, I saw Inch and some of his cohorts, looking visibly shaken, and concerned. They were under arrest in the holding cell.

"They took my car, Mick!" Riccardo said. "You know that I own a dealership now don't you?"

"Hell no! I didn't know that, what's the deal?"

"I can't have that car searched Mick-man! Inch said. I need to get that car and get the hell out of here."

I went to speak to the officer who had made the arrest and seized the car. Since Inch had not been fingerprinted, I could make the arrest go away as if it never happened. The question now was the car. "I have a good mind to tear it apart. "It is dirty!" The officer said. (Not to mention that the "VIN" number looks tampered with) I believe your cousin is in a stolen car business and is using the cars from his dealership to transport drugs." I told him that I was simply trying to do the right thing by family and that I would owe him one if he would grant me some professional courtesy and cut Inch and his boys loose and give them their car back. He did just that and never asked me for a favor or a dime in return.

Inch thanked me kindly and gave me a firm handshake. I always figured that by not putting me on, Inch felt as though he was protecting me. He did not want to see me get into trouble. I can not be mad at him for that. Six years later he was sentenced to thirty years in prison for criminal enterprising. I guess I should be thankful he did not take me with him.

Every hustle, I mean every street hustle that would make a man a dime in East Flatbush was already taken by other long established dirty cops. I had met a "pimp" named Mark who lived on Ralph Avenue with about ten girls, but he worked them in Manhattan and had no need for me. So kind and fearful pleasantries were all I got from him. With no money to be made, I decided to put my ear to the street. There is no better way to do that than by being a "skirt chaser". I would talk to every girl on the street, and if no money prospects arose, I would still get laid like crazy in the process.

I had gotten put on the midnight tour 2300 – 0735 (from 11:00 p.m. to 7:35 a.m.) and was partnered up with Willie Reed. We would park our RMP (Radio Patrol Car) outside of the Biltmore or Club Legend and talk to all of the girls we could. We would even bet on who would have the most phone numbers by the end of the night. We also met the rapper, Busta Rhymes. Willie was so impressed with Busta that soon after he went to work for him.

I convinced Willie that the Club Legend was the best place for us. There was a twenty-four hour diner across the street. We spent so much time there that I became friends with the cook and even cooked my own meals there. When the girls left the club, we would offer them rides home. Each of us spent many nights taking turns sitting in the RMP outside of some girl's building while the other one was having sex with her in his apartment. They were fun times and I cherished them. But at the time all I could think of was how broke I was.

Finally I broke Chilli-Pimp luck, and her name was Olivia. She was a dark Panamanian, absolutely beautiful, a stone fox. I saw her talking on a payphone on the corner of Snyder & Rogers Avenue. She told me she worked nights as a security guard in the Bronx. I had no reason myself to doubt her. We started dating like squares, like normal people I guess.

I had started off using a condom with Olivia, so it really didn't matter to me what she did. Since I wasn't judgmental and didn't pry into her personal life, she felt inclined to tell me that she was a working girl at Al's, Mr. Wedges in the Bronx. She was relieved to find out that I did not mind at all. I let her know that if she did not mind, I would come and see her there. That, of course, led me to driving her to and from work and eventually having sex with her at work. Olivia told me one day that her cousins, who worked at a different club, were going to start dancing at Mr. Wedges and that they would each pay me thirty dollars to drive the five of them (not including Olivia, of course) to and from the club every night.

One hundred and fifty bills a night sure wasn't solid pimp money and it was not hustle money by Brooklyn or anywhere else's standard, but it was a start. Olivia asked me if I could begin the next night. Sure, I said.

The next morning, I went to my trusted Nike Box and dug into my "stash ash" that I had accumulated from doing any and every kind of hustle, from robbing drug dealers to robbing the homes of people who had died after the County Medical Examiner had their bodies removed. I went to the dealership on Utica Avenue and brought a white Cadillac that looked more modern than it was. I ran to a "chop shop" shops I knew of and got me some rims that damn near cost me half of what the car did. I was hoping that this would turn into some big time pimping outside of

my career as a police officer.

The extra money I got from the girls was a big help even though they worked only three

maybe four nights a week at best. They always got seventy-five dollars from management just

for coming. So at the very worst we split the money almost even. I used this opportunity, of

course, to meet some of the women who were working there. It made Olivia jealous. I told her I

was trying to recruit and that she had some nerve being jealous, given that she did lap dances all

night. "Recruit for what?" Olivia snapped. We ain't got no room in our car!"

"Our car? First of all there is no 'OUR CAR'. Secondly, there will be no us if you keep

talking with that tone."

I added: "These girls in here think that I'm ya'll pimp." I told her to go on with what she

was doing and to tell her cousins to speak highly of me to the other dancers and tell them how

great it was to be with me.

"My cousins know that you're a cop Mick-man." Olivia said. I told her that she and her

cousins should be the only ones to know that. I figured it was a good a time as any to hip Olivia

to my plan for making some real coin.

I told Olivia to introduce me to every dancer, especially those who turned "tricks."

I had drinks and interviewed potential prospects throughout the night. I knew that in

doing so, I was upsetting the atmosphere and ruffling the feathers of pimps who were trying to be

inconspicuous in and around the club.

I did this for two nights. After I had a "quickie" with Olivia in the back area by the pool

table, I came out the bar and to Carmen, Olivia's cousin. She told me that some men seated at the table wanted to have a drink and to talk with me. I could see that they were pimps. It sent vibes. I

pulled myself together, I told Olivia to be on my right arm and Carmen, on my left. With their

four cousins in tow, I was escorted to the table. I realized that to behave in any other way than

cool would blow it. After I was seated, they dismissed their girls and I dismissed mine. I was just

glad that my girls did not make anyone aware that I was not what I appeared to be; not in the

slightest. In fact, I didn't even know what the hell to say. So I found it best to listen as carefully

as possible.

As they introduced themselves, I expected to hear names like "Kool Breeze", "Pimpin

Stan," names with flavor and color. But three of them were named: Steve-O; Mike; and Blaze.

As I extended my hand, my mind raced to find a name to call myself. I couldn't find one

that would be dramatic without being so over the top that would sound corny. So I settled with

my nickname, which had evolved from my childhood and is the result of my huge ears. They

resembled mouseketeer ears, and so I was originally christened "Mickey Mouse" by my closest

relatives. That evolved to Mick-Mick, then to Mick-man as I matured into manhood. I figured

the name I already had would have to do. Besides, I don't think anyone else on earth has it. I said

it to Steve-O first. He asked me to repeat it. That made my Adams Apple feel the size of a tennis

ball. I took a deep breath, trying as hard as I could to be cool and to belong. These were the kind

of men I had admired my whole life.

They were not working suckers who slaved for a living, just to turn their cheeks to some

evil Jezebel who was openly using them and probably giving the money to another man anyway.

They were not the big drug dealers who had so many women that they could not keep count of

them and basically kept them like trophy show pieces. They weren't the billionaire CEO's who had wives half their ages who knew that, sooner or later, but probably sooner, they would be taken to court and have the shit sued out of them for child support, alimony, palimony and everything else her lawyer could think of. Last and least, they were not the cops who were nothing more than meal tickets to the women who knew cops had fragile inflated egos, but were good for at least 17 percent of their seemingly steady paycheck, if she could just stroke his childish/cowboy ego long enough to conceive his child.

No, they were pimps and I was proud and honored to be invited to sit with them! I carefully thumbed through my mental notebook of everything Janice Quick had taught me. I sat stone faced, refusing to show teeth. I resolved that I would convince these men that I was a pimp, or die trying .

"What you drink?" Steve-O asked.

"Jack and Coke," I replied, trying to seem unfazed by the whole scene. Steve-O broke the ice by asking me that question, so I assumed that he was the "Boss Player."

"You gonna try and touch down out here in the Point with your girls?" asked Steve-O. "If the weather is right," I answered. I don't know how hot it is up here. I figured I'd test the water first by having them dance while I get a feel of the terrain." I said this to make him feel as though it was the police and only the police I was worried about.

"Well there's always room for more players on the field." Steve-O said. "We got no problem with you working your girls here in Hunts Point."

He said it with a sly grin, knowing that I was pretending not to be worried about him or any of the other pimps. I didn't even realize that I had allowed these men to put me on the spot.

I had talked the game. Now, I was expected to show it. Moaning that I had not put my girls out on the street because I had not been given the green light was no longer an excuse.

This was a tight spot to be in, especially since I had no working girls to begin with. None

of us were even in the life. I was a cop. Olivia was a student as well as my girlfriend, who was

stripping to get by. Her five cousins were all squares trying to subsidize their meager wages by

stripping and lap dancing. I had put us all in jeopardy of losing the crumbs we were getting just

to look like a pimp to pimps whom I knew had ways of testing you out to see how real you are

before the drink they ordered in your honor even arrives in front of you. I also knew that if I did

manage to convince Olivia and her cousins to work the streets I would most certainly lose my

job.

At that moment, I realized that this was my shot at the big time, so I might as well go for

it. At worst, I could keep my job. At best I would get rich in the pimp game and use the money to

fulfill my dream of owning a liquor store. I told Olivia to have her cousins meet me by the pool

table. They all came huffing, puffing and complaining.

"What is it now, nigger?" One of the girls said. I got people who want a lap dance. As I

was talking to them, I notice that the three pimps were now sitting with their girls and all eyes

were on me. They watched me intentionally court with my girls.

"Yall want to make some real money tonight?" I said.

"Do you know of a better club?" asked Carmen.

"Nah, baby I mean real money"

"Whatchu mean, hoing?" Carmen asked again, looking at me with venom.

"It's real money."

"Oh! So you went over there and sat with the wizard of oz and asked for some heart,"

Carmen said sarcastically. "Now you want to pimp?"

I noticed that Carmen said this with the look of someone being insulted, stunned and offended, but she also looked impressed. I noticed too, that she looked at me differently, not like the harmless cute little cop who was moonlighting as a cab driver for strippers, but like a man.

But Olivia and the other four looked at me with disgust. Olivia said, "I'll deal with you at the end of the night."

I felt that the three pimps had heard the whole exchange and felt humiliated. I went to the bathroom and tried to pull myself together. I looked in the mirror and said, "What the hell, I never would have known had I not tried." I figured I might as well play the night out. If worse comes to worse, I don't know any of these people and can resume my job tomorrow like this never happened. No one on the police department would be the wiser.

As I came out, I saw my girls sitting with Steve-O, Mike and Blaze, talking, smiling and drinking with them. That is all but Carmen. I looked around the room until I saw her; she was giving a dude a lap dance. She waved at me and blew me a kiss. I needed that.

I walked pass, making eye contact and nodding to Steve-O, Mike and Blaze, who were shouting daggers of death at my girls. Till this day I don't know why. I guess for a few minutes I felt like their pimp. Why? Because other pimps made me feel like I was. Pimps sure know how to work magic. If they can make a man go from feeling like a king to a slave in a few minutes, imagine what they can do to a woman. Pure magic.

I walked past them, holding my head high. I tried not to hate knowing that I would be breaking one of the golden rules of pimping by doing so. I walked out to my white Cadillac, which was nothing more to me now than a glorified cab, and sat down behind the wheel. I remember hearing the song "Cupid" by the group 112 on the radio, and I did all I could not to cry.

A few times throughout that night, I would peak my head inside the club, trying desperately to look like a pimp who was concerned about his ladies. Each time I looked in I saw the three pimps displaying power over their girls by ordering them around and so forth. I wanted that power in the worst way. I realized it then, as I know it now, that I did not want to pimp for the money. I wanted their kind of power over women. The money is just a by-product or proof of that power. Truth is, I would probably do it for free if I had no bills to pay. I wanted so badly just to walk up to Steve-O and beg him to teach me the magic, teach me game, bless me with the gift that he had, but that is just not how the game goes. I had started with these women as a boyfriend of their cousin and as their cab driver, and I knew that how you start off with a woman is usually how you're gonna end up unless you really impress them with a dramatic display of heart, which usually signifies extreme change.

I sat in my car the rest of the night. It seemed like forever until it was four o'clock. At that time all of the props of the midnight sporting life were ready to turn in to avoid the sun looking like vampires who were hell bent on doing as much damage to them as possible. They all filed out of Al's, Mr. Wedges, some fast and some slow. All the girls had to wait for the patrons to leave to receive their seventy-five dollars. I sat in my car ashamed to look anyone in the face. I felt as if everyone had seen what had happened to me and I could not stand the embarrassment.

All the girls walked to my car quietly; expecting me to say something nasty, snippy, and to act like a scolded square. I felt as though the worse thing that you can do when someone wounds you deeply, is to not show it. Even if you let them know it. A woman respects a weak man and a man who can't control his feelings is weak.

The first thing I did was notice that Olivia's cousin's Desire was not with them. I asked if she was O.K. and should I check on her. "No, she done let one of those pimps convince her to do a private party at this time of the morning for God's sake," Olivia said.

I said nothing more about her. "Ya'll want some breakfast?" I asked. No thank you, they all said sheepishly trying to guess at what I was thinking.

Olivia always sat in the middle of the front seat right next to me and would kiss me and molest me all the way back to Brooklyn. Not tonight! When she went to put her hand on my penis, I gently moved it, all the while talking very nicely to them, I looked in the rearview mirror and Carmen was giving me the sexiest look I had ever seen. Olivia said, "Oh yeah, drop Carmen and me off at Carmen's house after you've dropped off everyone else. Carmen wants to talk to you."

"I guess it's over between us, huh?" said Olivia.

"Yes it is", I said firmly.

Carmen never took her eyes off me as we drove to her house. All three of us walked up the parlor floor steps of her brownstone and stood there waiting for Olivia to get the message. Olivia looked down and with a respectful move squeezed pass and went inside.

"So you wanna pimp huh?" Carmen said.

"Yes I do." I said.

"Why didn't you just say that from the start?" Carmen said.

"I don't know." I said.

"You should always say what you really want. You never know.....Somebody might give it to you." Carmen said. "I want to make that big money too, except I want to be my man's only

woman. I want him only concerned about me. After all you are a cop and don't have time for a

stable. I know where to go to get big money too. Just me and you, I don't want any of my

cousins to know especially Olivia. You just watch my back, be in my corner and be there for me

when I need you. Can you do that; are you really ready for that?"

"Yes, I am," I said.

"What time you picking me up tomorrow?"

"Midnight"

"Where's my money?" Carmen demanded.

"What money?"

"You just chose me as your man didn't you?" I nodded.

"Then all that you have is mine," she said.

Carmen reached into her Louie Vuitton bag and handed me all of her rolled up wrinkled

little singles and fives and pouted her lips.

"That's all I have, daddy." Carmen said.

"Then that's all I want."

"You know your woman has had a long night and needs some affection." Carmen said.

"I'm your man right?"

"Yes daddy." Carmen said.

"Then that's my job"

As I went into Carmen's room I heard her and Olivia arguing in the foyer. Then I heard

the door slam. Olivia lived a few houses away, but after her refusal to back my play at the club, I never wanted to speak to her again.

Carmen and I started kissing in her parlor floor bedroom. I remember wishing that Olivia could see us. I sat on the bed and watched her drop to the floor what little clothes she had on. Carmen stood about 5'7" and was darker (a deep chocolate kind of dark, like a Hershey bar) then Olivia. Her body still glittered and looked like part of her dancing attire. She smelled musky and ripe from a long night of dancing. She wanted to take a shower first because she felt insecure about the smell. I wanted her to shower because she had been touched by so many men and God knows what else. As for the musky smell, for me it is a woman's natural fragrance of pheromone *(stimulus to other individuals of the same species for one or more behavioral responses)*, and I like it. But I wanted the man smell off of her, so a shower was a happy medium for both of us.

I wanted to really reach Carmen, please her and make her climax. I pulled some tricks out of my old Nobi Jones bag that left her bed soaked.

"What the hell is this, a chop shop?" I said, feeling very apprehensive.

"No, well I guess it is during the day but at night it's a club called The Goat," Carmen said assuring.

There were separate private rooms inside and an outdoor area. All the women were completely nude except for stiletto shoes and some belly chains. Carmen wore just a g-string, a long coat and some mean looking boots. After we sat down at a table, we both figured that she was way over dressed. Carmen simply stood up, took off her coat and stepped out of her g-string, handed them to me, kissed me and said: "Just sit tight baby. Mommy will handle the rest."

As she walked away, I could not help but notice her magnificent back side. I felt so proud that it was mine. I was no longer just a cop who moonlighted as a cab driver for some stripper. I only had one girl and that qualified me as a chilli-pimp. But, I had arrived; I was a bona-fide

pimp. I felt someone staring at me. I looked to my left a few tables over and Steve-O was sitting

there. He nodded to me with a look of respect that was worth more than all of the money in the

world to me. I ordered a drink and stole the moment. After all, a pimp is his own best company.

After about ten to fifteen minutes, Carmen showed up at my table and handed me one

hundred dollars. I could smell her "Coochie," it had been hard at work. I have noticed over the

years that one thing a working girl wants from her man is not to be judged, she expects

unconditional acceptance, especially when it comes the condition of her body, meaning that,

although she has been performing fellatio all night and her body may smell really raw, she is

your woman. She will not try to kiss you on the mouth because she knows where her mouth has

been and that you are not a homosexual. But she will attempt to hug you and to kiss you on the

cheek. As she approaches, she will make sure that you smell the Listerine or peroxide you have

given her, or try to at least. She returns but she expects your undivided acceptance of her in the

same way that you expect no hesitation from her when it comes to backing your play.

So after Carmen handed me my money and bent down to kiss me on my cheek, I stuck it

out for her to kiss. I hugged and caressed her gently while stroking her hair. Carmen then walked

toward the back room and melted into the light. We repeated this act numerous times throughout

the night.

By the end of the night, I was amazed to learn that Carmen had twenty one-hundred

dollars. It would have taken me a month to make that as a cop. I felt as though I had finally

arrived. Carmen never asked me for a specified amount of money. She said she was proud of

what she had made me. She then made a startling suggestion. If I were going to be pimp, then I should start to dress like one.

The next day we woke up very early, went to Orchard Street where one can buy more expensive clothes. We bought a white linen suit for one thousand dollars and a five hundred dollar pair of crocodile shoes. I was so happy. This was a dream come true. I gave five hundred dollars to Carmen. It would be us against the world, I told her.

As we walked toward The Goat that night, I noticed that we were getting got a lot of attention. After all, I was now wearing the "uniform" that made me recognizable as a pimp. The relationship that I forged with Carmen would be the blueprint for all relationships that followed. We were now best friends. We were real and honest with each other. We shared our likes and dislikes and our hopes and dreams, fantasies, pain and insecurities. We had a real bond, although I realized that the prototype of Carmen was Candy. Carmen allowed me to take such a relationship to the next level. We would take walks in the park, talk for hours while laying on the beach, travel together, try different foods in all kinds of restaurants that put together incredible money making schemes.

With me being a police officer it would have been too difficult to try and maintain a stable of girls. Still, Carmen tried repeatedly to introduce me to girls at The Goat who wanted to "come home with us." I guess I was just afraid of losing her. I was well aware of the dangers in bringing a girl home. Of all the threats she posed, the worst was stealing your girl away to a large stable of girls that was run by a very seasoned pimp, who could offer her better opportunities and luxuries than you could.

So I always refused. At this time in my life I was using my mother's address as my official address for job purposes, but I stayed most of my time at Carmen's on Martense Street.

With the money Carmen was making, I had enough money to handle her rent and the rent for my

mother's basement. I would stash money in the ceiling, in the floor, in my shoes and everywhere

I could in my mother's basement. My sisters would always break in while I was away. They

were not looking for money, strangely enough, but to steal my clothes. My sisters would wear

my baggy clothes and it made me mad as hell. But it just makes me laugh now. I never even

wore most of those clothes. I had Timberands and Jordans and what not that I only wore once, if

at all. I was just mad that they were broke in.

     Carmen and I would use the basement as a sort of cabin to escape the city sometimes. She

really understood me. She knew what I was thinking before I spoke. She would see me looking

at something while we were out walking, and it would be waiting or me on our bed when I came

home from work.

     It was the beginning of the rise of the third most corrupt police officer in New York City

history.

     When I was seven years old, New York City experienced its second black out in two

decades. The last thing I remember before the lights went out on July 13, 1977, was listening to

"Rockin' Robin" by the Jackson Five on a 45 record player my mother had purchased for my

sisters and I.

     We were on the third floor of 27 Cambridge Place in the front room facing the street

when Michael Jackson's voice started to slur. It sounded like "tweedy tweedy tweet tweeavda

deeaud deee."

     All of a sudden my sisters, my mother and me just sat there in the dark. We were

perpetually poor so we had no air conditioning. We had all of our gigantic brown stone windows on the third floor wide open so we could air. Within three seconds we heard not just a scream,

but a roar that could rival the reaction to a homerun being hit by Derek Jeter at the World Series.

My mother told us all immediately to get on the floor as she ran out of the room. In

seconds she returned with her service black .38 caliber special revolver. She came to the

windows and closed them. "Mommy, we burning up!" My sister Shana said. My mother spoke in

a calm voice, although I could tell she was near panic. "Shut the Fuuuuck Uuuup," she said. "I

will open them half way. I have to make sure no one tries to lower themselves from the roof into

our house and kill us all."

As she approached the windows, we could hear gun shots, sirens, screaming for mercy

and arguing. I can remember someone screaming, "Get off of me!"

"Get your fucking hands out of my pocket!"

That is when I realized the magnitude of our situation.

"Mommy, what are we going to do?" I said nervously.

"Nothing, but lay here quietly, stay alive and kill the first mother fucker that tries to get

in here." My mother said calmly.

After about two hours we heard pounding on our parlor floor front door. Throughout my

childhood whenever my mother became deadly serious she would always "cock" her gun. As the

pounding increased, I heard that famous cock.

"Like I said, y'all stay low." My mother said icy cold. She stalked through the darkness

like a mother leopard hell bent on protecting her kittens.

"Who the fuck is it?" she screamed out the window.

"It's your brother, Shay." My Uncle Tokey yelled up to the window. "Come on down, all the way down to the first floor, I need some help." His voice was very animated. My uncle was a

New York City Transit officer whom we all looked up to. He was my shining example of

everything a man can and should be. My mother looked up to him and so do I still to this day.

"Y'all go to sleep on the floor. I mean it!" my mother whispered. "Don't even move if

you hear a gun go off."

I woke up in the darkness about an hour later because of the serious banging and clanging

going on in my house. If I hadn't heard my mother and uncle laughing so loud, I would have had

died from fright. Although I had been told to stay put, I could not help it. I had to see what was

going on. As you the reader can probably imagine, a brownstone in the dark is about as dark and

scary as a haunted castle, but I had to see.

Once I was in the third floor hallway it was easy to see the first floor. I could see light,

but how? During the "Great Black out" my mother and uncle, put their job flashlights, as well as

two that we had in the house, on the sprinkler pipes tied to the ceiling, which really illuminated

the hallway. I could not believe my eyes. The hallway was filled with bikes; it seemed like fifty

bikes. There were also TVs, radios, and all kinds of valuable appliances including washing

machines. I mean, there was a treasure trove of merchandise.

My uncle looked at me while he stood surrounded by what looked like treasure of King

Tut's tomb. Dressed in his immaculate uniform, he said: "Come here and give me a hug

nephew," as he kissed me on the cheek. My father and uncle were the only men to kiss me on the

cheek. In return I kiss my four sons on the cheek as a sign of "fatherly affection." From that

moment on I wanted to be a police officer.

The problem was we looked up to him so much that it seemed unrealistic, like only one person per family could join the force. A good example of this would be, being President Barack

Obama's nephew. Just because he's president, does not mean you could be. But because of that

night, I never lost sight of it. I knew I was black and from Brooklyn, but I had to try.

In the middle of pimping and selling crack at the age of sixteen, I took the police test. My

mother thought it was a complete waste of time and that the NYPD would never call me.

She said: "First of all you're black, second you don't live on Long Island like your Uncle

Tokey and third you ain't the man my brother is! Your father ain't half the man my brother is

and he didn't have the balls to be a police officer. What makes you think you do?" My mother

was angry that I had the nerve to think that I was good as white people and for even thinking I

was good enough to be a cop.

I figured she was right but took the test any way. I kept on selling crack and pimping

whenever I could, all the while remembering my uncle and the stolen booty.

"If I ever do become a cop, I swear I will steal my ass off, like no cop has ever stolen

before." I would say to myself on an almost daily basis. I had no idea how prophetic that very

statement would later turn out to be. I did become the most corrupt police officer of my

generation.

There are several categories of cops. And then there are several categories within each

category. My personal belief is that it is designed that way so any one who has never been a cop

can not understand what the hell is going on within the police departments. Even other law

enforcement agencies, like corrections, parole, probation, courts, deputy sheriff's and even

sanitation police, would like to think they know what it is like to be a police officer or what goes

on in the police department. But in actuality they are as clueless as a New Zealand crickette player at an NBA All-Star game.

When someone becomes a police officer, he first learns that the way he looks, thinks and carries himself will determine not only who his friends are, but who he will work with, marry, party with and what career path he will take and with whom he will be on this path.

If you are black, you are immediately made aware that the glass ceiling is very real and that your avenues to advancement and even comfort are narrow. If you are black and move to Long Island and make it clear to all that you are only interested in dating white woman, then you stand a chance at least one day making sergeant. If you talk, cut your hair and even dress like a white man, then one day you might make lieutenant. If you are black and are not ashamed of it and show no outward self-hate, then even other black officers will not work with, talk to, or even eat with you in the lounge. This all starts as far back as the academy. I had a bigger problem then I thought I did not fit into a specific category. One would imagine that light skin black would be where I would be designated, but even I had a problem with that.

In week six of the police academy, all the recruits are told to go and join their fraternal organization, which are set up in different rooms on different floors in the police academy. I naturally went to the "Guardians" room, which was filled with my beautiful black sisters and brothers and was stopped at the front door as others squeezed passed me.

"What do you want?" One officer said.

"I'm here to join the Guardians." I said with pride.

"You have to be black first." Eric Adams said to me. He is now New York State Senator Eric Adams.

I was crushed, embarrassed and sheepishly walked away looking back at harsh stares from "my people".

I car pooled with three guys from Staten Island; David Diaz, Gaetano DiSamone and Michael Vinceguerra, all Italian and borderline Mafioso. I had attended Public School 204, so I was comfortable with them. I walked away from Eric Adams and the Black Guardians, I saw the three of them headed to the "Columbia" Italian Fraternity room. So I said to myself: "What the fuck, why not?"

To my surprise, I was allowed to enter and join. We were all told to write down exactly who was from Italy on a piece of paper and told a few jokes. I felt kind of good and a part of something that was weaned for becoming a police officer. I was paying the price on the outside world. All black cops do complete ostracization. All of my family and friends completely turned on me or looked at me with distrust. So this meeting was about the only time in my life where I felt like I belonged somewhere. That changed after graduation.

Once arriving on patrol and realizing that black cops who knew they were almost doomed to a life of watching E.D.P.'s (emotionally disturbed people) at the hospitals, sitting on bodies or DOA's until the meat wagon comes or walking the beat for 20 years. I thought back to the "black out" and told myself to stay focused; my time would come.

The three categories of corrupt cops are as follows: Grass Eater, Meat Eater and Omnivorous Shark.

A grass eater is someone who skips someone on the "row tow" log book to make a tow truck company next in line to tow an abandoned vehicle or a car you claim to be abandoned (wink wink), or eats at the same diner everyday "on the arm" or for free, or steals from the property locker from time to time. In general he is a petty criminal with a badge, a rookie (we all start off as grass eaters) who hasn't graduated to the big league yet, or just a loner who

systematically does petty crimes to get over the hump in between Thursdays (cops are paid every

other Thursday).

A meat eater rarely is a loner, because usually large scale crimes involve a crew who can

watch your back or intimidate. It's pretty hard to put the fear of death into a crew of vicious

criminals by yourself. The meat eat will not even speak to the cops outside of his circle. The

meat eater is consumed with paranoia and thinks everyone is a potential rat. The meat eater

changes his route home everyday and is afraid to talk on the phone. The meat eater is basically a

member of an organized crime organization within the police department, and he will often

display the characteristics of a "mafia" member.

The omnivorous shark is a strange bird indeed. Although he considers himself a loner, he

is very gregarious and charismatic. Everyone knows him, likes him, but fears him and distrusts

him. He smiles and laughs without smiling, even his smile is intimidating. Good cops shy away

from him and all cops shake his hand in fear. The omnivorous shark knows and bullies all street

criminals and takes whatever he wants from store owners.

The omnivorous shark eats grass and meat and steals for the sake of stealing, almost out

of boredom. He is reckless and seen by all as a "loose cannon," with a death wish. He is always

pushing the limits to see just how much shit he can get away with. He is usually the leader of a

meat eating crew and is expected to take the fall when the Feds swoop down and everyone's face

is on the news.

Since I was all alone in the beginning and had no friends, I decided that the only way to

get into a meat eating crew was to make myself into the crew.

After being a grass eater for a year in C-Pop walking foot post 1B on Church Avenue in Brooklyn's 67 Precinct, my chance finally came.

I was fine pimping and selling drugs outside the job but that was small potatoes. I wanted the big time to be part of the meat eating crew.

One day in the summer of 1996, I was eating a slice of pizza on the corner of Church Avenue and E. 34th Street. When I saw two cops run upon a white car and shoot a man 24 times. Jimmy and Kevin were part of a meat eating crew with serious connections and I wanted in. The guy they killed was one of America's Most Wanted and civil unrest ensued. The street was blocked off and I was part of the riot that followed. The white car was taken to the 6-7 precinct garage where Kevin, Jimmy and now Frank were tearing the car apart looking for a gun because they had shot an unarmed man 24 times, and cops are given just 48 hours to come up with a reason for killing someone.

Every cop watching this was told by Inspector Ray Powers to go either inside or on patrol. As we were all leaving, I asked Jimmy if I could speak to him. He motioned for me to come over. I asked if I could look into the car. These guys looked puzzled and pissed. After all I was black and not in their inner circle. As I was told to buzz the fuck off, I slipped a 9 millimeter under the seat where I knew they had already check and scurried away. 48 hours later the story was in the paper.

The headline read: "One of America's Most Wanted killed in fierce gun battle with cops in Brooklyn"

I was invited to T.J. Bentleys in Bay Ridge, Brooklyn by Kevin, Jimmy and Frank. I was in.

I was not the only one who saw them. Whenever a drug dealer did not want to pay me on Church Avenue, I would call whatever sector they were working via the radio, request that they go to Channel Nine, which was short frequency, then tell them to pay me a visit, which would be where they killed that guy. It would sound like this:

"Sector, Adam Boy on the air," I radioed in.

"Go ahead Goldie." Kevin said.

I would say: "Go to Channel 9."

When they were close enough they could hear me on Channel 9.

Once they were there, I would get in the car with them and we would pay a visit to whoever I wanted to terrorize. Afterwards, I would leave money wrapped in an envelope with a P.A.R. (police accident report) in their mailbox; every cop has one in every precinct.

After a series of crackdowns in Brooklyn, I got scared. I also had heard from a friend I had met through Jimmy that a ton of money was being made in Sugar Hill, Harlem, in the 3-0 precinct. On "Dirty Thirty" as they called it. I moved from an apartment I shared with three prostitutes I owned and moved up there as well. I fell in love with Harlem and still love it.

I got Jimmy to use his connections to have me assigned to Manhattan North Narcotics. I used everyone and everything as a resource or a lookout even without them knowing it. I actually made a friend while working there besides my friends, Wesly Trapp and Jack Checnak. Francis McCabe, was the only adult friend I had. Even though he was not corrupt, he would lie to cover for me even to his own peril. You see his father was a police legend and Frank knows what brotherhood was all about. He backed me up and would not hesitate to send someone to the morgue in the name of brotherhood. I would do the same for him. Frank was one of those old school cops who did not see black or white, right or wrong, Frank saw BLUE!

I was assigned to Franks' partner and would disappear with my crew, leaving Frank alone often. While I was being an omnivorous shark, Frank would patrol alone and always vouch for me. As the days, turned to weeks, months and years, Frank never gave me up and even gave me my name, "Candyman".

I would get tips on the street for days; I would watch certain drug dealers on my own time. Then, while on patrol, I would tell Frank to go 10-63 (meal). I would have Dominicans who were the rivals of the drug dealers and other dirty cops from the 2-5 precinct, transit police, district 3 and sometimes P.S. A-6 back me up.

I would wear my uniform (a few times I did not), I always carried a ski mask. Frank always asked me why, while laughing at me. I would rob the drug dealers either in an apartment or in a stair well, sometimes in a car.

Sometimes, I would get only a few thousand. A few times I got up to as much as five hundred thousand dollars. I needed carrying all that money away to my car. I parked right outside the precinct and would meet back up with my partner, Francis McCabe. We still joke about how I used to disappear like Houdini. Frank is still amazed I became a "most wanted" criminal in my own right by the D.E.A., F.B.I. and my nemesis Lieutenant Ernest Pappas. After two years of this I was starting to be called the "Prince of Harlem", which I liked a lot. More like LOVED IT!

They could not get to me. I was too isolated. I paid off bosses, their bosses and people in internal affairs. So I was yanked off of the streets and sent to Central Park. I was riding high on top of the world; I paid off the sergeants on the midnight tour and conducted business at One

Fish, Two Fish on 97th and Madison. I had three different drug crews making weekly payments of $20,000 or my people would shut them down.

There was a price to pay for this. I could not be touched, and Frank could. After constant harassment, Francis McCabe resigned in 1999 because of me. A good cop. The best and most honest I had ever known. I'm sorry Frank.

I also strained friendships of those who were very good to me, treated me like family. I would like to thank the Moncoe brothers of Lloyd Street, Brooklyn, New York. Richard and Lamont are my god brothers. I would park my personal cars in front of their house and stash my drugs and guns there (they had no idea about the guns and drugs or that some of the cars were stolen). Lam and Rich would keep an eye on my cars in between their tours as correction officers. I would even sleep in their house on cold days as a beat cop in Brooklyn. Had it not been for you two I would be serving life in prison. But I still wanted to be promoted and be a boss. *I was sentenced to an "A.C.D." a conditional discharge. If I were able to stay out of trouble for six months then my record would be sealed. I was later informed by the Deputy commissioner Ellen Swarz that I will always be remembered as the dirtiest Cop who never really got caught, and a*

career criminal without a criminal record, but a career criminal none the less.

I was still seriously trying to pursue advancement in the police department, believe it or not. So when a position opened up in Manhattan North Narcotics, I was elated. Would I not only make detective, which would give me more power to protect me and Carmen, but I would also be in a position to extort and steal millions of dollars of drugs and street money. Carmen and I talked about it and figured that it was an opportunity that I could not pass up. The sky would be the limit in Manhattan North Narcotics.

I was assigned to Harlem's Sugar Hill, the land of milk and honey. I was busy working all kinds of unpredictable hours, but was worried about Carmen working The Goat or other clubs alone. So I finally relented and let her bring a girl home. We interviewed several girls before settling on Stephanie. She was about 5'3", a one-hundred-sixty-five pounds brick stilthouse. She had hazel eyes and close cropped curly hair, which was so curly that they looked like a wig of big circles and loops. It went well, though. I told them to look after each other and made note that all of Stephanie's money remain in the possession of Carmen, Stephanie readily agreed.

Since I was being assigned to Harlem, it was no big thing to stop in on them in The Goat. Sometimes, I would come in uniform just to throw my weight around. It made the girls feel very safe while terrifying the pimps.

Each morning when I came home, Carmen and Stephanie would always throw a welcome home party for me. Sometimes, I would catch them "releasing some tension," as they call it. I would interrupt them and sit as if I was in shock, because when I busted my wife cheating with another woman. I would tell them to continue and then I would passionately make love. They would be listening to very sultry music. Carmen had an excellent music selection. My favorites were Michelle Indegeochello's "Here I sit outside your door"; Mary J. Blige's version of Roy Ayers, "Sunshine" as well as the Roy Ayers version; Heat Waves "Star of the Story", and my favorite at that time, "Brown Sugar" by D'Angelo.

As I got deeper and deeper into the hustling game in Harlem I would spend less and less with Carmen. I was relieved when I discovered that I had underestimated her. I kept worrying that she would choose another pimp; I had not figured that she would become a pimp herself. I paid the rent and all the bills so I maintained my control of Carmen, Stephanie and now Yvette.

There is one rule that I have learned in this lifetime that applies whether you are involved

the sporting life or if you are a square. That is, "If it ain't broke, don't fix it." All people have

certain wants and needs. If you find a way to conveniently combine them into a simple

combination, leave things as they are, or at least ride it out until everything goes bust.

I was so blinded by the money I was hustling from the street in Harlem that I all but

abandoned Carmen and the girls. I would drop in time to time to freak with them at Carmen's

house or at The Goat, but I was too stupid to see that I was blowing something special. Drug

money does not provide you with companionship, so you start dealing with girls that other drug

dealers deal with and they are mostly "gold-diggers".

Drug dealers are nothing more than squares with a connection, and they almost all get

snared by women who just want to be taken care of. Try as they may not to appear as squares,

deep down that is what they are, squares. They usually wind up being tricks because most of

them have no game.

The last time I saw Carmen she was in The Goat. She was wearing a Gucci sweat suit,

sneakers and a hat, as well as a ton of diamonds and gold. She had added two more girls to her

stable. Carmen took the girls down South and has been there since. I just wish her well and I

thanked her for everything. I was neck deep in the hustling game in Harlem and really didn't

mind.

By the time the rug was pulled out from under me in Harlem, I had gone through roughly

two million dollars and thought I couldn't be touched. To put it mildly I had gone mad with

power. To me everything and everyone was for sale. I was dealing with women who didn't care about me at all, and used money to replace my lost mojo that I had traded for in the first place. I

was arrested in uniform as other officers clapped and applauded. I was lead out of the precinct by

a dozen Internal Affairs Officers as well as a half dozen FBI Agents.

Until I could finish with my criminal trial, as well as my department trial, I would be on

modified duty assigned to the Criminal Justice Bureau in Brooklyn, or in laymen's terms, the

Brooklyn Central Booking.

While working there, I really missed Carmen and the whole sporting life. So when I

noticed that I would be working by the female cells, I was excited. Maybe I would see some

familiar faces, I thought.

At first, all I saw was crack heads, dope fiends, the drug regulars of society. Then they

announced that there would be a crackdown on prostitution and that we would get ready to work

a lot of overtime handling the girls brought in on the prostitution sting operations we had on the

streets and in clubs.

I saw hundreds of girls I knew from the Rose M. Singer Center on Riker's Island, from

the Forbel Female Detention Center in Brooklyn, from the Ward's Island Correctional Institution

for women and the Elmhurst Mental Ward. A lot of them were dope fiends and always dope sick

or kicking, as we put it. I used these girls to convince the incoming prostitutes that I was alright

and could be trusted.

One day, while sick as a dog, one of them said, "Please, a lollipop, a piece of candy,

something sweet, please!" I ran to the store and got her a lollipop. Sure enough, she stopped

vomiting to the point she could talk to me. From that moment on, I would keep lollipops and

hard candy on me at all times. The Candyman of Central Booking was born.

I had missed the company of working girls so much that I would check the cells constantly to see if there were any working girls in them. As I came in to work, I would even ask: "Any prostitution stings last night?" I loved it most when there were at least twenty of them in the holding cell. I didn't mind, even when there was only one. I would always break the ice with a piece of candy and a cigarette, then would talk her ears off all night.

Sometimes a girl told me her whole life story while crying out loud. I would get the keys and let her out, hug her and let her sit at the desk with me instead of in the cell. Sometimes I would tell a girl my story, and she would cry on my shoulder.

One night about ten, girl from the East New York "track" were bought in to Central Booking. Their main corner was Stanley & Georgia Avenues in a desolate area between Pennsylvania Avenue and the Brooklyn Housing Project. The girls and I hit it off right away. The ringleader turned out to be the "bottom" women of this particular stable. Her name was Diane Washington, but everyone called her "Juicy."

Juicy was extremely concerned. She asked me, exasperated: "That motherfucker Karopkin out there?"

"How's that?" I replied.

"The Judge" she answered annoyed.

"I'll go see." I assured her, I asked which court would be having night court and if that same judge would be arraigning the prostitutes.

I found out that the misdemeanor court stayed open until approximately 9:30 p.m. Any remaining misdemeanor cases would go to felony court, where that court would arraign all the cases it could until 1:00 a.m. I also found out that all of the prostitutes hated Judge Karopkin, I guess because in turn he hated them. He would sentence every girl to ten days, which meant lost

wages for the prostitute, which meant that there would be one furious pimp waiting for her when

she got out.

"So why would she ask me if Judge Karopkin was out there," I thought to myself. I went

back to the female cells and called out "Ms. Washington." She came to the gate looking

aggravated.

"He's out there, Juicy"

"He is?"

"If I made it so you didn't see him, what would happen?" I asked.

Her face grew excited. "I'm in here too early right now, usually when they bust us if we

find a way to stall at the precinct by the time we got down here we go to the felony side and that

Judge loves us. He'll give us community service that we never go to or he'll have us "R.O.R"

(released on your own recognizance). "Could you find a way for us to see the felony Judge.......

Candyman?"

"Giving me the names of the girls she wanted cut loose." I took the "rap sheets" of

Sesame Seed, Midnight, Foxy Brown, Peaches, Dimples, Honey, Storm, Fire, Passion and of

course, Juicy. I went to the movement elevator that we used to transport the prisoners to the tenth

floor and the corrections department where the transfer of custody took place. I stopped the

elevator on the seventh floor, which was empty and wasn't used for anything except to tune-up

prisoners or have sex with prostitutes, or at least it was what my fellow officers used it for.

I dropped all of the rap sheets down the elevator shaft. No paperwork, No court. The girls

would even have to take their mug shot again. I did feel bad about one thing. The female civilian matron who took care of the girls got in trouble for the lost paperwork. But thank God she did not know that it was me who stole them while a girl distracted her with a fake epileptic fit.

My tour ended at 11:35 p.m., and before I left, I stopped by to check on Juicy and the girls who were left, being taken out to get their mug shots taken. They all screamed: "Candyman! That's my man!" Stuff like that. It felt good to be appreciated and to be able to help.

The next night, when I came into work at about 6:30, I was advised that I had some interesting people waiting to speak with me on State Street at the ramp behind the courthouse. They were two extremely good looking women who said that they were instructed to take me out and show me a good time for the favor I had done for them the night before. I told them that it was not necessary and that I was just glad to help. Storm and Foxy Brown told me that they were given the night off to do so because I had saved their pimp two weeks worth of money and they would get into trouble if they did not make me happy.

I went to my Sergeant, who was very cool, and asked for lost time; time that's accrued on your account. For example, *for every 5 days you work, you accrue 3 hours of lost time that you can use if your Sergeant allows you to.*

My Sergeant agreed and off I went with these two beautiful girls. I did not have any money but women have a way of making you feel rich when you do not have a dime. They treated me to my favorite restaurant, the "View", on 44th and Broadway. After playing footsie with the two of them under the table, they escorted me to the dance floor. I loved the attention I got from onlookers who gawked at me strutting through that posh spinning restaurant with a woman on each arm and downstairs to the spinning dance floor. We danced and laughed and had a wonderful time.

After getting pretty drunk, the girls, one on each arm, of course, escorted me downstairs to get a room. I used my ID but they paid for it. I was sober enough to remember to wear a condom, thank God, and we made love in a beautiful room until the sun came up.

What felt best about it all was that I did not ask for it. I guess my heart was in the right place when I helped those girls and something wonderful happened to me in return. It was a nice time in the middle of the storm my life was going through at that time, and to tell the truth, they really wet my appetite for life. I wanted to get some money, maybe not like what I was getting in Harlem but more than what I had at the moment. I would have to make lemonade out of limes and make lemonade I did.

I was assigned to the cells in the sub-basement or intake where the prisoners first come from the precincts into the system. In this assignment, you strip search everyone who comes in. We were not supposed to let them keep more than one hundred dollars on their person. I broke rule number one. I let them keep all the money, figured that relieving them of it would be easy. I would sell them luxuries during their two, three and sometimes four day stay in the slammer.

I was required to take all their cigarettes from them. I, of course, sold them back for extremely inflated prices, and our sick junkie problem become solved. When I first arrived at BCB, the smell of vomit filled the air. Heroin addicts would vomit their guts out while waiting for God to help them. They would also shit their pants at the same time. This was very unpleasant; I came up with a very simple solution, I would sell them heroin! This gave the male prisoners a reason to call me Candyman as well. To further link my pockets, I turned off all the water fountains and sold sodas for five dollars a piece. To make sure I covered all the bases, I kept blow and weed in my locker to help out anyone hurting for the "girl and the dirt".

Three different pimps would routinely meet me on State Street and pay me five hundred

dollars a piece whenever their girls got busted to make sure they didn't go to jail.

By this time I was feeling quite like myself again, except that my gun and shield were

gone, which weakened my ability to influence and corrupt people on the outside. Without my job

I had no power of influence, which meant no big money. I started planning ways to make

contacts in case I lost my job while exhausting all means of getting money while I still had this

influence.

I was served with numerous notifications to appear in traffic court in Harlem for

hundreds of moving violations that I wrote on people while assigned to Manhattan North

Narcotics. Each and every time I went I would be early, I would seek out the people who I had

ticketed and offered them an opportunity to have a severe case of amnesia in front of the traffic

judge for a small fee. I made a fortune.

As expected, I was fired that spring. I would have to tough it out as best as I could until

some contacts I had made were released from prison. I know I could survive, but pimping and

hustling would never again be as fun. Yet, in return I would be free, meaning I could just be a

pimp or a hustler or whatever I wanted, and I would not have to hide it anymore. Shit, I could

even wear a beard and dress like huggy bear if I wanted to. I felt like the sky could be the limit,

then I decided against it, figuring that the best hustlers hid behind legitimacy. So I would

continue asI had been.

Chapter Eight

"The Phoenix"

I was like the Phoenix who must completely burn to complete destruction before it could be reborn from the ashes. After 10 years of law enforcement, every person or every hustle I was involved with was connected to my job as a police officer. Everyone around me was afraid to deal with me and everyone acted as though, by cutting those out, somehow I could get my job back. It would be just like in the movies; all I expected was to be able to carry on my criminal enterprise as business as usual.

To my surprise, I was comfortable being clean cut, happy to be drug and alcohol free. I did not expect it but my very approach to crime changed dramatically. I went from conducting wide ranging criminal conspiracies that involved lots of people in numerous states to doing day to day completely solo survival crimes. Meanwhile, my parents gave me, my child and my child's mother three months to get myself on my feet. Then I had to get out of their basement.

My son's mother got a job at McDonald's on Bay Street in Staten Island. She spent a lot of time there, which gave me a lot of time with my son, which caused us to really bond. My focus really came into view at this time. I had to make a life of crime all on my own with the limited contacts I had and I had to act fast.

My neighbor Keith had just been fired from the Teamsters Union Local 825 where his uncle was a huge powerhouse. I did not think he was worried though because it was about his seventh time being fired. Keith approached me when I was sitting in my mother's yard with my son one day and asked if I could score him some blow. Do not worry about the price, he said. He would pay whatever priced I asked and would tip heavily for door to door service. I got a hold of an old friend and got a line of cocaine going.

I had Keith as my sole customer but I could not keep him supplied enough. I then turned him to my close friend Alicia Bing who could not handle him. We still made money with what little coke we had, but our supply could not meet his demand. Keith then turned to another childhood friend of ours, who was an Italian mobster based in Northern New Jersey who had an endless supply to sell Keith. I lived next door so I still was able to make money due to Keith's impatience and laziness.

Everything seemed to be going alright until I heard that Keith was found dead in his parent's home. I felt terrible. I did not sell him the coke that killed him and I did not turn him on to drugs, but I still felt bad. I also felt confused, Keith was Irish, and from a good home. He had well connected parents who got him a job and were in his corner. Why was he so unhappy? I still ponder that fact to this day. While Keith was drowning himself in blow and trying to get his job back with the Teamsters, he worked for Ralph's Pizzeria on Post Avenue. When he died, I tried to ask for his job. I knew Ralph would never hire a black man, but I still tried. That just goes to show you white people have all the opportunity in the world; we blacks have none.

With Keith gone, things took a dramatic turn for the worse. My parents, who were friends with Keith's parents, somehow felt as though I contributed to his addiction and ultimately his death and wanted me out even sooner than the few months they had given me.

When my parents went to work the next day, I threw a yard sale, and sold all of my expensive clothes. Some of the clothes I had never worn. I sold my $500 crocodile shoes for $5. I sold everything except my computer. I ultimately made about twelve bucks. All the clothes I did not sell I threw away. All other valuables were put in a stolen shopping cart from Pathmark. I pushed the cart with my son in the front seat all around my neighborhood I looked like the character from the wire named "Bubbles." I was just glad my son did not know what was going on at the time.

I finally sold my computer for four hundred dollars to the Arabs who owned a grocery store on Decker Avenue. I also sold my clock radio and a few other knickknacks that bought that day's total to damn near six hundred dollars. I used that money to apply for jobs, police and otherwise across the country. I also took my son and ex-wife to New Orleans for a three-day Police Hiring Program where applicants are given a series of tests, medical exams and so forth. Approximately two weeks later by phone, you know whether you have the job as a police officer or not.

I was still lying to myself at this point, trying to convince myself that I could make it in this world legitimately. After coming home and getting the bad news from New Orleans, my son's mother got sick and was unable to work. My mother demanded that we leave post haste. I was dead broke and in a jam. Then my son got sick, food poisoning from old beans in my cabinet. I felt directly responsible. It was life or death. His mother and I slept in the hospital room with him. I remember crying as they slept.

All the people who I had looked out for when I was a cop were nowhere to be found. All the favors that I had done for people were not going to be returned. Everyone I knew did not care whether my son lived or died. I quietly begged God for my son's life, and in my mind, I made a deal with him. Please give my son a clean, healthy life and please allow me to show them Godly things. In return, I would not ask for mercy for me on Judgment Day. I would gladly accept my fate in hell, not for all the things that I had done but for the things that I was about to do. After a week and a half, the IV was taken off and my son lived.

The next week, I moved my son and his mother to her apartment in Harlem. I checked into a Route 1 & 9 hotel in New Jersey and started selling weight at a slightly higher price to a few good friends in the Montgomery Houses in Jersey City. A few cops who were enemies of mine and were waiting patiently for me to be fired, felt as though now was the time to make their move. I was followed out of Harlem, over the George Washington Bridge, down the NJ Turnpike to Exit 15E, Communipaw Avenue, and then northbound on Route 440. My cell phone was not working, so I stopped to use the payphone outside of the Wonder Bagel's. I was approached from behind and told to turn around; I spun as fast as I could and got a hold of the gun with my left hand pulling straight down, the gun discharged and I was shot. After a brief struggle the would-be off-duty police assassins gave up and ran because of all the attention I brought to us by screaming my head off. The sound of the shot was so loud that I lost part of my hearing in my left ear. Sometimes I still hear ringing.

I crawled back to my car and drove around frantically asking people for the closest hospital. I finally found Jersey City Medical Center. I parked my car right outside the emergency room and crawled inside. The problem was not that my nerves were severed, my bones smashed and ligaments ripped in my lower left leg. It was the amount of blood that I had lost. I almost

died; I had to stay a while in the hospital to make things even better. I spoke to friends back in

Harlem and I was told I could not come back, that I had no place there. I made a few phone calls

and found out that a friend of mine needed someone to drive ecstasy from Chicago through

Minneapolis and across the Canadian Border to Thunder. I could earn $1,000 a week for making

the run twice a week.

Chapter Nine

"Chicago – Graduate School of Crime"

When it comes to hustle, Brooklyn and Chicago differ in several ways. A Brooklyn hustler is more like a hyena, a scavenger taking advantage of any and every angle or prey it can. When it does find prey, he devours the whole carcass down to the hair and toe nails. A Chicago hustler is a specialized predator who not only makes money in one arena but is proud of it and strives to be the best hustler in his game. He takes pride in his title, and those of them who are true to their game, believe or not, will turn down money he can make from any other hustle even if it comes easier.

For example, a Chicago pimp would never settle for being a Chilli-Pimp. He would constantly strive to be a boss player. A Chicago pimp would not want to be involved in any other game than the pimp game because he firmly believes there is no money like ho-money. A Chicago pimp wants to wear the pimp uniform; he's in it for the long haul. I mean these guys are really dedicated. They are always planning and scheming to stay one step ahead of everyone that can impede their progress, which makes Chicago hustlers and pimps more like foxes than hyenas.

Chicago pimps and hustlers have lineage, meaning generations of them have passed down game and cons for over a hundred years. Chicago hustlers and pimps choose their games while we wind up in ours after finding ourselves on the street trying to eat. That is why we end up trying our hands in several games.

As I said, Chicago is a traditional place with old bloodlines and established territory.

Anyone who believes he is going to just touch down there and head out with his girls to the nearest track without permission, authorization or protection is crazy.

I had a plan I thought might work. It would mean bigger things if done on a small level. None of my schemes, dreams and best laid plans would have come into fruitation without the help of a dependable strong black woman, and this instance was be no different. Tamisha Jones was a very interesting woman, to say the least, and was the best friend a man could ask for, the perfect confidant, who would not rat on you even if blindfolded in front of a firing squad. Tamisha trusted her life to me. She preferred to be called Jonesy because she was a lesbian, bull dyke as some people refer to her kind. Tamisha wore corn rows and dressed like a man, but she was still attractive.

Jonesy and I were as thick as thieves during my time in Chicago. We made numerous trips together to Canada, Minneapolis, Cleveland, and to New York by car and Greyhound. Jonesy. She was a teacher to me; she taught me all about female psychology. I watched her constantly. She did things and said things and sometimes behaved in ways that to this day I do not understand. Jonesy and I would go out to regular clubs as well as strip clubs. Although Jonesy would dress like a man when we went out, she would get jealous of a girl playing me too close, and sometimes she would get jealous of me because she liked the girl I was talking to.

Sometimes after dressing like a man for weeks, she would show up at my hotel suite dressed like a woman. She would be very attractive, almost unrecognizable. During those weeks with her dressed like a man, we behaved just like two male friends would act; calling each other homie, my nigga, giving each other a pound, and stuff like that. Then out of nowhere I would be standing on a corner talking to some "money people," and she would come switching and swaying up to me, rising her up high over both of our heads, pressing her body very seductively up against in a way it said: "that's my baby". She would then embrace me very sexually and give me a kiss on the lips. It was very confusing, I know. And contrary to what most people thought during my stay in Chicago, I never had sex with Jonesy. I could not and can not have sex with any woman who behaves like a man, even if it's only part-time.

Jonesy confided to me that she wanted children and was willing to let a man have sex with her for that purpose. After all, she was female. I watched her a lot and noticed all kinds of hypocrisy in her actions and words and did not know whether she was confused or if she was intentionally trying to confuse me. Without a doubt, one thing she knew was women. She could look at a girl for a few moments and know all about her. She would even tell me just what to say and how to behave with certain women, as well as what to look out for. Yeah, she was an expert at reading females.

Jonesy would leave me with her car when I first came to Chicago, and ride public transportation. She would sacrifice for me and never told me why. Jonesy would never let me hold the door open for her because it made her look soft. But when we rode the Greyhound for twenty-two hours to New York to deliver some guns we bought at an East Peroia Gun Show, she cuddled up with me like a kitten. People stared at us because she was in her corn row gang banger outfit. As she slept on the bus, I would look up at people smile and shyly say, "It's a girl." When Jonesy woke up, she would apologize and say she did not mean to lay on me and caress me and would ask me if she said anything to me in her sleep.

Jonesy and I both knew that the military paid the first and fifteenth of each month. We also knew that there was a huge naval training center in Great Lakes about twenty minutes to the north of us. Military men and women are legendary for patronizing professional women of

leisure. So we thought we would try our hand by going to the chicks near the base, as we had

drove to the clubs in and around downtown Chicago.

In no time we had a few girls out on our own little make shift track and was pulling in

some decent money. I never had to check Jonesy, meaning, I never had to put her in her place

because Jonesy was an expert "bottom woman." She worked those girls damn near to death. I

can still hear her singing, Snoop Dogg's "I stay on point like Stacy Adams." She loved that song.

On top of all that, the best thing she did for me was listen. I told Jonesy my life story and

she absorbed every word. She counseled, comforted me and mothered me. For someone who

seemed to dedicate, her ultimate skill was doing only what the purest of women do, and that is

bring the best out of a man.

One day, Jonesy said that she had a surprise for me. I waited for her at my barber shop in

Waukegan. wondering what it could be. She drove all the way down Interstate 94 and we talked

about the usual stuff: money, hoes and clothes. She pulled up to the Cabrini Greene Housing

Projects, a tall building where the Evans family lived in the TV Show "Good Times" I said:

"How did you know I was such a big fan of that show?"

Jonesy said, "Are you kidding? You watched it all the time? I thought you should see it

before they finish tearing the building down."

She then continued telling me all about the city's history. She told me all about Larry

Hoover and the Black Gangster Disciples; Jeff Forte and the Black P Stone Rangers. She drove

me out to the most famous track in our nation, just west of Cabrini. Green is the track of the Arch

Bishop Don Magic Juan, the most famous pimp of our generation. I was informed by one of our girls "Red" that when asking about him, ask for the wizard. When stepping out of the car, all the

girls averted their eyes from me, scurrying in every direction, which is classic behavior when

working girls recognize a pimp is in their presence. It's frustrating at first but boosts your ego in

the end. After this happens to you, you'll say to yourself: "At least they know a pimp when they

see one."

So of course I used Jonesy to speak to them. They told her that Don Juan was in

California doing professional entertainer stuff with Snoop Dogg and that he would be back at the

end of the week. I was disappointed. I wanted to shake his hand, hoping that some of the magic

would rub off on me and that I would become the greatest pimp who ever lived. I felt good,

though, knowing that I saw his track.

Jonesy showed me Curtis Mayfield Way, the Loope, the Sears Tower, and Lakeshore

Drive, the site of the Saint Valentine's Day massacre and numerous other landmarks and

attractions. While eating a Chicago deep dish pizza, Jonesy says to me out of nowhere, "You

smile too much," I asked her what she meant.

"Some people feel as though you're weak because you appear to be a happy go lucky

kind of man and not a mean ass pimp. Especially when you speak to women, try not to smile

even when you're telling a joke… just try it and see what happens". She was right!

The four girls we had working for us seemed happy to be working for not just us but to

be representing me. They want their man to be a real mud kicking, ass kicking no nonsense

pimp. Jonesy also talked about the history of the game and how it started during the

reconstruction period after slavery when sharecroppers started leaving Mississippi and coming

up the Mississippi River and stopping at all the Riverboat towns along the way.

Jonesy talked about how the modern stroll method using a track was first done in Memphis, Tennessee, before making its way to Chicago, where it was perfected. Coming from New York, I always thought that being a pimp required you to be able to talk a mile a minute and be able to maneuver people to do what you wanted them to do..

Jonesy taught me that the trick was to be needed by her, to listen to her, to be a rock in her corner, and to discipline her when need be, not to just put the gorilla hand down because she is short five dollars.

Jonesy talked nothing but game to me for months, she knew everything about me, too. She even reminded me to send money to my son every week and sometimes did it without telling me. Needing to be closer to my son was becoming an issue for me. Chicago was just a tad bit too far from my son in Harlem. I missed him terribly. I proposed to Jonesy that we move East, maybe to DC; or Virginia or Atlantic City area. Jonesy told me that she would go wherever I wanted her to go and would make damn sure that all the girls came too. I felt that once again my life was just about perfect except one piece of the puzzle just did not fit. I wanted to be a father as well as a pimp and hustler. I figured I would be able to pimp and hustle as long as it was done on a small scale. I also knew that if I did it too small I would blow the girls and maybe even Jonesy as my bottom woman, or as I called her, my underboss.

After stacking money and going with the flow for a few months, I made my decision. I had to be closer to my son." I also decided to go back East alone. I had made some calls to reliable contacts that made me feel safe in other parts of the city at least to come and go but not live.

Jonesy cried and asked what in the world were she and the girls to do. I looked deep into her eyes and said, "No one knows the game as well as you." These girls are now yours. I'm only

a phone call away if you ever need to talk or to have me come out here or to wire money or

whatever. You'll be just fine, Mr. Jones!"

The day I left she hugged me harder than any woman ever has. All the girls gave me a big

group hug, too. When I say all, I mean all four; I was still a chilli-pimp in my eyes. I would not

have had four had it not been for Jonesy.

Chapter Ten

"Virginia – An Unknown Treasure"

There really are no tracks as far as I know in Virginia, just a ton of strip clubs, a few

resorts, and a state with very relaxed gun laws. Jonesy had taught me how to go to gun shows

and make "straw" purchases; that is, to get someone with has a Virginia license to buy the guns

for you.

After talking to family and contacts and securing a place of residence, I decided to put the chilli-pimp and the Brooklyn hustle to work on a small and steady scale. I mean small to allow me to see my son on the weekends and to spend quality time with him. If I used the Chesapeake Bay Bridge and tunnel, I could be in New York in seven hours, assuming, that is where the guns are. So I would be able to, in essence, get paid while seeing my son.

I checked in at Heartbreakers on Mercury Boulevard. in Newport News and Hammerheads in Virginia Beach. I found a girl who was looking for a place to stay who knew the lay of the land, and most of all, knew how to turn tricks at the Virginia Beach Resort Hotels.

Tina was a young naive coke head who thought she knew everything. After being broken in and properly checked, she fell right in line. She was a very dark skin, lean but curvaceous country girl who had bowed-legs and walked pigeon toed. Her face resembled that of someone with an Asian background. As long as she was coked up, she was ready for whatever appeared. This was not traditional pimping, to say the least, but it suited my needs. All week long, we would either sit on Yorktown Beach during the day or picnic in what seemed to be hundreds of state parks. At night, she would work the strip clubs or the resorts, and sometimes even the regular clubs. One time I took her up to the Paper Moon in Richmond, just for a change of pace. The money she made helped buy guns at pawnshops in Portsmouth, Virginia. I would get at least $400 a night from Tina. I would then buy four guns from a pawn shop in Brooklyn for $800 a piece. Everyone wanted one, even some cops I knew from my Brooklyn days. That's $100 paid out and $3,200 coming back in. That was for the simple 380's. Once I started bringing back M-16's, Calico's, 30 aut 6's, the money really started rolling.

I started off making one trip a week. Then I began to make two. You should never have just one girl working. She needs a partner, someone she is comfortable with but does not really

know that well, so they can watch each other's backs. That's another 'Jonesy' rule that makes for

a happy house and increased profits.

After a few interviews and auditions we settled in, Tracy was another coke head, so she

and Tina got along pretty well. We worked this program for eight months. I stayed with my son

at my sister Shana's house on the weekends my son and I were bonding well.

That summer we went to Great Adventures in Jackson, New Jersey, six times and the

Bronx Zoo twice. We saw every children's movie that came out. I showered him with love and

presents and felt as if leaving Jonesy was the right choice.

I took Tina and Tracy to Atlantic City for a vacation as a reward for the outstanding job

they had been doing. The three of us fell in love with the place. Since I was moving so many

guns, it would be a good idea to put some distance between myself and Virginia anyway so that

Federal and not local law enforcement would be all that I had to worry about. The feds were not

worried about a small time pimp and small time gunrunner, believe you me.

Chapter Eleven

"Atlantic City – Chilli Pimpin"

We moved into the Howard Johnsons on Pacific Avenue. Several years earlier my family,

the "Cook" family, were one of the biggest black families in America, especially when

accompanied by our cousins, the "Love's", now known as the "Cook-Love Family". They had

hosted a reunion there and the hospitality room was the suite. I liked it then, so now I was going

to live there.

A pimp named Dollar Bill had the most lucrative part of the track, from the Taj Mahal, which was South Virginia Avenue, to South New York Avenue. He had a pretty respectable

stable of about eight girls. Outlaws and girls who belonged to Chilli-Pimps worked in front of

the Martinique across from the Howard Johnson's. There was a track in front of the bar,

"Herman's. It looked really busy, too, but that made me nervous. If you went north of South

Virginia Avenue, you made yourself vulnerable to the locals who lived in that housing project

right up the street.

I knew that prostitution was tolerated by local law enforcement because it boosted

tourism. All the police care about in Atlantic City are the casinos, of course, but more

geographically from the boardwalk to Pacific Avenue from Black Horse Pike to the Taj Mahal.

This is where the white tourist generally stay while visiting Atlantic City.

If you stepped one foot away from Pacific Avenue in any direction away from the area I

just described and if you are not white, your ass is grass. I decided that where we lived was the

safest place for Tina and Tracy to work.

I quickly wrote down all the numbers and addresses I needed to know. He is most versed

in where he could find his girls when they vanished. Whatever local central booking, police

precinct, county jail, hospital and morgue, you make sure you get your girls paid, as well as get

them cell phones, condoms and disinfectant spray for their vaginas, mouthwash, and hand

sanitizer. You inform them of all the traditional rules as well and the few others of your own. I

took them shopping to buy their working clothes, and a few items that simply make them happy.

When you go to a new place, it gives the pimp an opportunity to strengthen their bond with the

girls in the hope that some local pimp does not whisper the right combination in her ear that puts

her under "his spell" and put her in his stable.

After spending the day shopping, eating, gambling and checking the town out with the girls, the three of us made hard passionate love back at our suite. As the night fell, I saw the other girls come out to Pacific Avenue and I knew it was time. I had the girls dress in their uniforms and I put on mine.

While in Philadelphia visiting my cousins; Rodney and Perry on the South Side, I had purchased an all white linen suit, green and brown gators and extra gawdy bracelets with raised rings. I also cleaned my gun and made sure that my police credentials were in order. I planned not to stray from the Police Gray Zone, so I would not have to worry about getting robbed. But I did not want to be recognized as a pimp by the police either, so I planned to mostly stay in my car and only raise myself when I wanted to be recognized by other pimps.

After about two hours of Tina and Tracy jumping in and out of cars on the side streets off of Pacific Avenue across from the casinos, they both flagged me. One of them said: "It's good out here daddy, but there's a lot of competition. We all thought we could make more money if we worked in the casinos, just as we had done with the resorts in Virginia Beach."

I said, "The money is why we're here, go get it then." I sat in my car on Pacific Avenue, while they went into the Tropicana. After about an hour and a half, I flagged Tina and asked where in the hell they were and why had not they come back outside after not breaking luck for so long.

"Because we working our asses of daddy, there's a ton of money in here and all the other ho's on the street". One of them said.

I parked my car and came in to see what the hell was going on. Tina was talking to a guy at a slot machine and Tracy was on her way, arm and arm to the bathroom with a blue collar looking white guy. Tina excused herself from the mark and came up to me beaming and proud.

"We are making a killing daddy. We done turn about ten tricks a piece in the last hour-and-a-

half."

"Ya'll made ya'll quota for the night?" I asked.

"No, not yet daddy, but we will in no time," Tina said.

"Then it ain't that good in here," I said, as if I expected better from them and really was

not impressed.

"O.K. it's about 11:00 o'clock right now," I said. "Y'all do y'all thing and call me at 5:00

to come in, if and only if, y'all money is right. Y'all can come in."

"O.K., daddy we'll do fine," Tina said.

I spun on my heels feeling pretty good about myself and damn near starved from hunger.

We were in such a rush settling in, I had not had time to eat. I was not even sure of where to go

to eat. So I drove around just taking in the city.

I decided on the Atlantic City Bar and Grill on Pacific and South Carolina avenues. I sat

at the 2nd floor dining level up against the wood wall in front of the bar. So I had a pretty good

view of who came to and went for the bar. I placed my order and was waiting patiently when

Dollar Bill sat down across from me. I asked: "What up pimp?" I just sat stone faced, wondering

how long he had been following me. I decided not to be confrontational or deny that I was a

pimp. Instead, I explained exactly where I stood on the food chain in the hope he would state his

territory and welcome me to New Jersey.

"I just touched down today." I said. He abruptly interrupted with, "I know." I started to

wonder if my life was in jeopardy. I coolly continued. "I just got two girls and I…..". He interrupted again, "I know that, too."

"What do you want from me Dollar Bill?" He smiled wickedly at me. "I own everything from South Virginia to South New York on Pacific Avenue. If I catch one of your girls reckless eyeballing, she will have to come out of pocket. You're fine to do the same to mine, but you'll never catch one of mine out of pocket."

Dollar Bill checked me out from head to toe looking for flaws. I mean he was not checking to see if my clothing was authentic; that would also be a flaw. Besides everything on your body being of the highest standard in pimpdom, it can not look as if it is breaking you to dress the part; your attire has to look effortless. You almost have to look as if you wouldn't care if someone threw a glass of red wine on your eight-hundred dollar pants because you have a closet full of them. Your jewelry has to look comfortable on your hands, wrists and neck. Even though they are very gawdy and they must look as though you wear them to sleep, and must look like they are cleaned daily.

Dollar Bill nodded when he looked at my shoes and gave a respectful nod when he looked at my three-sixty waves; his waves roped just as bumpy and had fresh line.

"All you do is pimp?" He said, as though I looked as if I was earning more than standard chilli-pimp pay.

"I'm down here layin' low," I said, as if I was confiding in him. I heard it was open down here. I ain't trying to be 'boss player;' I'm just trying to eat."

"We'll see how you do," he said. "In a few days maybe we'll hang out. Have you met some player from A.C.?"

"Thank you, I appreciate it." I said, knowing damn well that there would be a snow storm in hell and that the devil would go ice skating before I hung out with this shark.

"What do they call you player?" Dollar Bill said.

"Candyman," I said.

"I know," he said in a jokingly manner but seriously trying to give me the impression that he knew all, I better keep my game tight. He then stood up and placed a one hundred dollar bill on the table and told me to enjoy my meal. I thanked him kindly and told him I looked forward to returning the favor.

I ate what I could, considered the situation and then went back to my suite. I wondered how the girls were doing and hoped they were alright. I had a feeling that Dollar Bill was not representing himself but, in letting, a group of pimps, which made our situation very delicate. Not being able to rest, I decided to spy on him as much as I could. He was so on top of things that it seemed I would not be able to get the jump on him. I also wanted to know if he was for real or if he was inflating his position on the track. I might as well take his in than to test his table because he damn sure was going to test mine.

I drove up to front of the "Grotto", the strip club right in the middle of his territory. I saw three girls. There were they were standing by the curb and looking into cars as they drove and came to a crawl to leer at the girls. As I approached, I looked at all of them with a deadly stare. They all looked to be damn near in terror and scurried away. I called after them. The more I called, the faster they moved. I got that bitter sweet feeling again; one of rejection with power. I hated the rejection but loved being recognized as a pimp.

I went to the door of the club and was met by the low budget looking door man.

"Who's the boss pimp out here?" I said.

"Dollar Bill," the doorman said.

I stood quiet. "You coming in?" the doorman said. I left. At least Dollar Bill would know

that I was for real and had not high tailed it out of town.

I could see the three girls had came back with another three. None of them made eye

contact but they let their presence be known. When I got across the street, the doorman said out

loud, "That nigger ain't sayin' nothing slick."

I was appalled by their rudeness but unmoved. I went back to my suite and declared

round one a draw. I rested, freshened up and went back out around four to check on the track and

see how Dollar Bill marked his territory. I saw a bunch of working girls in front of the Grotto,

some of them were sitting defiantly. The door was closed and none of Dollar Bills girls were out

there.

I pulled the car right up to them; they all looked away but one.

"Candyman is that you?" she said.

"Juicy!" I said.

"It sure is good to see you." Juicy said. "These bitches is scared of us. They don't it from

Brooklyn out here."

Juicy and her crew from Brooklyn had scared away the girls, the patrons, the tricks, and

the doorman, who was cowering inside. I figured it would be a good thing if everyone saw Juicy

and three other girls get in my car. Which was just a gold Toyota Camry with BBS rims, but it

still would look good for Dollar Bill to hear not only that I had checked his girls but also they

came back for seconds to pick up three girls from the only strip joint right in the middle of his territory.

"Get in girls!" I said.

"Juicy, ain't he a pimp?" One of the girls said.

"We can't ride with him," One of the girls declared sticking to the code.

"Candyman, You sho' nuff pimpin' now?" Juicy said. "You ain't a cop no more?"

The girls began to panic repeating what she had said loud. At that point even Juicy got

nervous and told all of them to pile in the back as she climbed in the front. I had never met the

other three, so I guessed that they were recent "turn outs" of Juicy. "It's fifty for a blow and one

twenty-five for a fuck," said one.

"Shut up, bitch! He ain't no trick," said Juicy, defending my honor. "So he is a pimp!

Juicy, what the fuck we doing?"

"He used to look out for me and my girls back home, I don't know if he a pimp or not, let

me see." Juicy said.

"Candyman what's good baby? Tell us the deal". Juicy said.

I drove off slowly and began to tell my story as best as I could without panicking them. I

figured as long as I was seen driving off with them, the impression on the track I desired would

be well received.

Four blocks away and still on Pacific Avenue, I was pulled over. At first I was nervous.

After all, I had a car loaded down with four girls who would be recognized as nothing else but

street walking prostitutes. The girls all gasped, "Oh My God, Big Kawala is gonna kill us," one

of them said. I calmly took my gun out of my pocket, let Juicy see it and put it under my seat.

The cops let us sit for a while with the bright high beams and the overheads on us until two other cars arrived. Then two officers approached each side of my car with guns drawn.

"I haven't met you yet," the officer said. You think you can just move your bitches into Atlantic City pimp? It ain't that easy!"

"Excuse me, sir?" I said, trying to look as confused and innocent as possible. "NYPD Manhattan North Narcotics. I'm on vacation and ran into my cousin Diana Washington, whom I haven't seen I years. Ain't that right girl?" I handed the cop my old ID card that I had claimed was lost before I was fired. Juicy pulled her ID out, and, sure enough it said, Diana Washington."

"OK, officer have a good time and be safe," the cop said, with a devilish grin as he gave us our ID's back. We drove three more blocks and then pulled into the parking lot of the Martinique, the hotel of the outlaws. "Candyman, we can't understand this town. Can you please give us the rundown on A.C. and you?" said Juicy, frustrated, shaken and impressed.

I responded firmly as I could with a cold demeanor, "First off, introduce the stable."

"Oh, this Passion, Cherokee and Pinky."

"How ya'll feelin' ladies?" I said as deep and concentrated as I could. They all said in unison, "Fiiiiiinnnneee, Candymaaaaan". I told them that I had gotten hurt on the job and had received three quarters disability, so I had technically retired. I told them that I was breaking into the game and had two girls. As I was telling them that, all the smiles left of their faces. I told them that I was new to A.C. and had just gotten there that afternoon and that here were two tracks as far as I know: Pacific Avenue and the block in front of "Herman's", the bar.

Juicy told me that Big Kawala had sent her down there with the girls to scout the area and see if they could make any money. "He trusts you like that?" I said not believing that any pimp's game was that tight that he could send his bottom woman this far away and that none of them would stray and his money would be right. I began to think that maybe I could get them under

my thumb. "If y'all ain't touch down nowhere, I got a suite here, and like I said, I'm trying to

break into the game." I told them. All you got to do is choose. Juicy you know I'll be in your

corner and the other new women here. I'm bona fide and qualified."

Juicy spun and stared at all three of their dumbfounded faces with a murderous stare and

told them to get out of the car. At first I thought they were mystified by my pimp game. In a

minute I learned that they were mystified by my stupidity. When it was just Juicy and I alone,

she said, "First of all, I told you I was the bottom bitch, you don't try to pull us all at once. You

are undermining my position, I guess you are trying to get in the game. Anyway, I don't like this

town; it was just me, Passion and Pinky. I just got Cherokee to choose me tonight". I looked at

her in disbelief, "That's right. She's one of Dollar Bill's ho's and she chose me." Juicy said.

Juicy then told me that it was not a good idea to stay in Atlantic City because Cherokee

pulled her coat to Dollar Bills rep and it was corroborated by outlaws on the street. I then asked

her where she was heading. "Big Kawala told us to head to Baltimore if it wasn't good here". I

tried to assure her that was best for them, that we could become millionaires, that I could protect

them from Dollar Bill and that life would be beautiful. I also told her that I always loved her and

thought about her night and day since I saw her last.

Juicy's face got deadly serious as she said in a very husky voice, "Candyman, if you were

a trick, I would fuck the shit out of you…..but you're not. You really are trying to break into the

game. I'm in love with Big Kawala and I'm his woman and bottom bitch. It took me a long time

to be his bottom bitch and I plan to do right by my man. Now can you please take us to the

Greyhound Bus Station?"

I drove them there in silence. I finally realized the pimp's true worth can only be measured by the quality of his women. I wished them all well, as they walked into the station. Cherokee was hugged up and under Juicy's spell. I knew that Juicy would be able to handle herself if Dollar Bill showed up on some player hating shit. Man! I wondered what my stable would look like and how much money I would make if I really could pull Juicy or a woman like her.

Big Kawala was one lucky pimp, I thought as I drove off. Or maybe it was not luck. Maybe if your game is strong, you can create a woman like Juicy. Maybe, just maybe, the stronger your game, the stronger your bottom woman and your stable.

That thought made me feel optimistic about my future in Atlantic City. I said out loud, "PIMP HARD, BIG KAWALA! PIMP HARD!"

At around 5:00 a.m. my phone rang on cue. I was parked outside of the Tropicana so all the girls had to do was come outside. They looked worn out as they climbed into the car and I smelled saliva and raw beaten pussy. The smell was so strong that it burned the hairs in my nose. I said, "Mmmm hmmm, I love that smell. It smells like money."

"Yes daddy, we did good tonight," said Tina, as she handed me my quota for both of them. It was a modest eight hundred dollars. It was our understanding that everything they made past the quota was theirs, which encouraged them to work hard.

I drove to a diner and bought breakfast to go. When we got back to the suite, I gave the girls a bath with beads and female products I had purchased while I was out that day. When they were both finished bathing and eating, I rubbed lotion on their backs and feet and we had light conversation about current events, R&B singers and stuff like that to make them feel like we had a connection, that we were a team, a family. Some pimps like to have sex with their girls at the

end of every night. And some have sex with the girls that give them the most money as a reward.

But when you're a chilli-pimp, you try to cater to their needs, meaning that if the girls are tired

and you got your money, reward them with pleasantries. You still keep a firm hand. You do not

ask them if they are sleepy. You tell them they look sleepy, to go to sleep.

The next day was mellowed, we all slept hard. While Tina and Tracy slept really late, I

went to the Spanish restaurant on Atlantic Avenue and bought lunch. When I got back, Tina was

in the shower and Tracy was lying on the bed watching TV.

"Hi, daddy!" Tracy said with a seductive smile, as if to imply that we should take

advantage of the opportunity to have some private time together while Tina was in the shower. I

had no reason not to give it to her. So far, she had kept up her end of the agreement. So I put the

food down on the coffee table and sat down next to it. I saw and smelled that she had just

showered and douched. That relieved and relaxed me. The last couple of days had been rather

tense. I was never one who liked to receive fellatio, but I sure enjoyed giving cunnilingus. So I

just enjoyed myself, I got so into it that I did not even know Tina was sitting on Tracy's face

after what seemed like only a few minutes.

After letting off some serious steam with both of them, I took a shower. But not before

carefully removing the condom and pissing. Urinating is very important to a male's hygiene

especially when dealing in a high risk environment like the one I was living in.

After my shower, we sat down together and ate. We had light conversation and planned

the evening. I felt as though the street was where they belonged. I somehow felt as if we were

cheating by going on to the casino floors. Tracy suggested that it would help a lot if I would try and procure them customers from the bar, or anywhere for that matter, where I felt comfortable. I

assured them that we were all in this together and that I would, in fact, procure all that I could for

the cause. But first, I wanted them on Pacific Avenue if nothing else for the formality of it. I

strongly believed that working girls belonged on the street.

I saw the worry on their faces and knew they were afraid of Dollar Bill and his girls. I

looked at them and said, " I'll be there. I wanted to make the point that we would go wherever

the fuck we wanted." I did not want to press the issue too much. After all, if the money was

inside then. That is where we had to go. Money is money.

I could see that they both were hurting for blow. They had that twitch and were

constantly puckering and curling their lips. I decided to take care of that problem immediately.

We all drove to exit 5 on the turnpike to see my family in Burlington. Their noses were raw by

the time we got back to Atlantic City. I also kept a stash after that to keep them well and

whenever they didn't feel right. I, of course, would never use blow, not even at gunpoint.

The girls nervously walked out onto Pacific Avenue at the Southern end of Dollar Bills

track. Both broke luck after a few minutes. When getting out of the tricks cars, I saw some of

Dollar Bills girls coming toward them. I got out of the car hoping to catch one of them

"recklessly eyeballing," but to no avail. They scurried away, looking at the ground (damn I loved

that feeling). In no time I saw Dollar Bill with about four girls in his burgundy Mitsubishi

Montero fly up and "mad dog my girls," but they did not take the bait. He drove away

screaming, "Stay off my track, I'm warning you!"

I figured we had made our point and headed to the Tropicana. The girls were relieved.

They went to hunt tricks, and so did I. I didn't put my heart into it though. I just feel comfortable talking to men about sex of any kind. I did my best to have a trick or two on standby whenever

one of them was not scoring. Believe me, when I tell you they did not need my help at all. Those

girls were doing their thing. They were going up to rooms and back down like crazy. I should

have figured that we would attract negative attention in no time.

Hotel security approached me at about 2:00 a.m. and insisted that I take my hos and do

business elsewhere. I called Tina and Tracy on their cell phones and instructed them to pull up

and meet me at my car which was at a designated location in the parking lot of the El Grecco.

When we all got into the car. We knew we needed a new plan of action. I wanted to leave town

but did not really know where to go. I thought about Baltimore but then dismissed it, mostly

because I knew that Juicy was there and I felt as if she could steal my girls at will. I thought

about Philadelphia and then about the violence associated with it, especially by the Muslims

who hate our entire way of life. I always feel like this when I get noticed by any law enforcement

entity private or municipal.

When I was a police officer, I always took note of what happened to hustlers of any kind

who brought attention to themselves. Once they were known, it was only a matter of time. Law

enforcement always does its best to take down a black hustler with a dime in his pocket, not

because of any ill that is being done to the community, not because of his lack of morale

character, not because of any victims of victimless crimes, but because of the most racist reason

of all…. He is black and has a dime in his pocket.

As they say, hindsight is always 20/20. I was very little brain and mostly cock and balls

and was stupid enough to play games of cat and mouse. By writing this book, I guess I still am. I

thought that I could stall for time by working every casino on the four-mile boardwalk. Dollar

Bill would not be so patient. The first place I tried was the Taj Mahal on the very outskirts of

Dollar Bills' territory. We went in at about 3:30 a.m. and were approached by the police and

security at 3:50. I identified myself to the Atlantic City Police as a retired cop and was allowed

to leave with my girlfriend and her cousin. As we went pass the street level buffet and up the

escalators to the boardwalk level, I felt totally defeated. I looked at all that purple carpeting and

that giant chandelier and said to myself: "The white man is never going to let me have any of this

shit. I will always work for him in one form or another. I will either arrest innocent black people

and plant drugs on them for him or I will sell drugs to black people for him. I will sell my

women to him, all the while risking my freedom. So while he enjoys all of it, I enjoy none of it.

The worst part of it all was the prospect of my son and future children being fatherless.

At the top of the escalator, Tina and Tracy, my comrades in this war, could see that I was

troubled. They grabbed my arm as we started walking. I saw Dollar Bills flanked by two goons,

leaning up against the wall near the elevators, smirking at us. I said out loud, "We just gonna

have to work the streets. That's all." I looked back and his smirk was gone. I touched the girls

down in front of the Howard Johnson's, which was right on the southern tip of Dollar Bills track,

I knew it would bother him, and foolishly, maybe I liked it. I sat in my car and watched the girls

come and go. At times, they looked nervously at me to make sure I was watching them. If I was

paying attention, they were safe. It felt good to know they knew that they were safe with me. I

made sure that I was armed to the teeth in that car. I did not feel like a pimp watching his ladies;

I felt like a commando in an armored tank.

After about a month of standing watch all night, I grew restless. I figured that maybe

Dollar Bill had given up his war with me and would allow my girls and me to exist on our little corner. I desperately needed to see my son. I had come to New Jersey to be close to him anyway.

It was summertime and the New Jersey State Fair was coming to the Meadowlands. I knew my

son would love it. I thought about making the girls lay up in our suite while I was gone. Then I

decided against it. I told the girls not to go anywhere but just to do "in and outs", to turn tricks in

cars around the corner from the hotel and to watch each other's backs. I left them with enough

"get high" to last a couple of days. I left my instructions and blow with Tina. Even though there

was only two of them Tina was officially my bottom woman.

I sure loved spending time with my son. We rode the sky tram, and all the kiddie rides

that he could stand and ate all the cotton candy, zeppoles, and sweets that his little stomach could

handle. I saw that he was starting to favor me and I began to wonder what he would be when he

grew up. Would I be alive when he did? I started to feel that I needed stability as well as security.

I felt that full-time chilli-pimpin could not be a life long thing for me. Although it's one of the

safest hustles, it is very time consuming and not conducive to raising a family. I was aware that

of the great ones who had done it, such as Bishop Legrand from Brooklyn. He is recognized as

one of the all time greats and I give him the upmost respect. I never saw myself on his plateau

which is probably why I have never been there.

I went back to Atlantic City feeling very upbeat and optimistic but, that feeling would

soon change. "That bitch is showing signs of cross daddy!" Tina said. She was pissed and

holding court with Tracy while I listened like an impartial judge to all the facts and testimony

before an imposing judgment. "First, the bitch kept disappearing on Friday night! Tina

explained. Then she didn't come home at 5:00 a.m. Come to find out she was laying up with one

of Dollar Bills' bitches. I couldn't get a hold of the bitch until noon, and then she disappeared on

Saturday night again!"

I felt the noose tightening I was just glad that Tina was as loyal as she was or I might have come home to nothing. Tina and I spoke alone outside while Tracy sat on the bed, waiting to see what we would decide. We decided that it would be best for Tracy not to be on the street at all. Tina said that she would do all the leg work for a couple of days.

At least Dollar Bill gave me the respect of making it formal. I had done exactly what he expected me to do. Tracy and I sat in the car in front of Howard Johnson's as Tina broke her first luck of the night. We sat there for no more than ten minutes before Dollar Bill drove up and got out of his jeep with two of his girls in tow. They stood on the corner as if they were attempting to claim it. I got out of the car, approached Dollar Bill and said: "Look you told me your track ended across the street. That means that this here is neutral ground."

Dollar Bill looked at me as if to say, "you don't know what the fuck is going on face." Then he yelled: "Your girl is reckless eyeballing. She owes me money!"

I said, "Nigger, she ain't even working. She don't owe you shit!" Dollar Bill got calm and said, "So you ain't playing by the rules huh?"

I said, "What the fuck you saying?"

Dollar Bill sighed and said, "Why don't you let her choose whom she wants to work for." Even to this day, writing about this makes me mad and embarrassed. My first response was to explode with extreme violence. I had never been in this position before. I looked over to Tracy who actually rolled her eyes at me. I walked over to the car and told her to get the fuck out! "You choosing right now!" I said. She nodded, half stunned, I said, "Then choose!" She walked over to Dollar Bill and his two girls. One of the girls hugged her and said, "You home now, baby. I'll take care of you." I stood there ashamed and enraged as they walked back to the car, I felt like a

man left at the altar. As they drove off, I looked at Tracy. But she did not make eye contact with

me. None of the girls did. Dollar Bill, on the other hand, looked square into my eyes. I stared

with a silent burning fury within, the same way Denzel Washington looked at the colonel in the

movie 'Glory' as he was getting whipped. I did not cry, but I sure as hell felt like it.

I was feeling like my manhood had been taken away, when Tina walked up to my car and

got in. "Some bitches just don't know a good man when they have one," she said. "But not me

baby. I'm in it for the long haul."

At that moment I felt good again. That's the real power of a woman. She has the power to

make a slave feel like a king. A woman can visit a man on death row and through a glass box

make him feel free and secure in their relationship. I think that the divine creator himself

designed it this way; it sure serves a purpose. Thank you God for the power and beauty of

women!

I told Tina that she could take the rest of the night off, but she insisted on working, citing

that we needed the extra money. I told her that everything she made that night was hers.

"No daddy ...... it's ours," Tina said. As she walked off into traffic I got choked up

vowing to kill anyone who gave her a hard time.

Chapter 12

"Chilli-Pimp or Brooklyn Hustle"

Six days went by very smoothly. I got to know Tina. She became my Nobi, my Candy, my Jonesy, and my Juicy. I even got to the point where I would get jealous when she walked off

with a trick. She knew it too. Women always know. She would wink at me and mouth "I love

you daddy." I felt like I could not stand it if I lost her to Dollar Bill. When I could, I followed

Dollar Bill and the two thugs watching his back just to learn his patterns so I would kill his ass, if

given the chance, if he fucked with my Tina.

Three days later, I had food waiting for Tina at 5:00 a.m. but she did not return. Tina had

assured me she could handle herself. So I loosened up the reigns. But I knew that something was

wrong right away, I felt it.

I left out of the suite at about 6:30 a.m. and started looking everywhere, police

headquarters, the hospital, the morgue, every inch of every casino, every store, I walked into the

twenty-four hour strip clubs, asking all the girls if they had seen her. I did not slow down until

about 5:00 p.m. I figure it would not be long before the night people came out. So maybe I

should rest before calling around again to see if she showed up anywhere. I called Tracy, her

phone was disconnected. Dollar Bill had covered all the bases.

I spent the night covering my search trail over and over in my mind; still no Tina. I was

really worried. I really needed the help of the woman of the night. Since they never made eye

contact with me before, I had the feeling they would not now and I was right. They tended to

their trade and frantically avoided me.

After a week looking for Tina, day in and out, I was exhausted and it showed. Gone was

my confident swagger and air of invincibility. I knew that it was standard practice in resort towns

like Atlantic City to starve chilli-pimps out if they could not "peel them". By this I mean, they

kidnap your girl and hold her up in a room. You would eventually go broke (especially if you could not cop another girl) and would have to leave town.

I knew there was one last person I would have to ask. I just wanted to leave him with a message not to hurt Tina. For not doing so, I would leave town.

I pulled up to his jeep. He was alone, I asked if he had a minute. He smiled and said, "Sure playa." He pulled over. I approached him with my hand stretched out in surrender, the same way the head coach does after losing the Super Bowl. He was dressed immaculately, looking the very image of what a pimp on top of his game should be. His haircut was so fresh he had powder on his neck. He was dressed in all white linen, his jewelry was fresh from a cleaning at a jewelry shop. His dollar green gators were fresh out the box. It all looked effortless. Well done, I thought to myself.

I, on the other hand, looked thrown together and was a sweaty mess. To make it worse, I needed a haircut. I sighed and said: "Look Dollar, my girl is missing. I just don't want her hurt. If she chooses someone else, that's fine. Those are the rules. But I got to make a stand if she's snatched. Since I'm in no position to do that, I will leave town in the hope that if I do she will be allowed to go back to her mother's. If I can, I'll even leave money with you for her to get her home."

Dollar Bill looked at me and I could see he felt sorry for me. I had totally surrendered to him, which kind of spoiled his celebratory mood. He had expected me to go kicking and screaming into the night, or possibly even getting killed over "pimp pride." He looked at me with pity and said, "I haven't seen her, I'll ask all of my girls. If she turns up, I'll give her your message."

I was convinced he was lying, but was powerless in this situation. I then offered him money to give to her for her trip home, if she turned up. "No need player," he said. I'll just tell her to call home. That's if she turns up."

I said, "Alright, then I'm gone, You own the stage." Walking off in defeat and doing my best not to slouch, I heard: "Candyman." I looked back at Dollar Bill. "She'll be alright." He reassured. "Don't worry." I nodded and left town. I hoped I had saved her life. I kept thinking and thought about what happened to her and I felt terrible.

I went to New York and rented a room from relatives. I sat by the phone for days, but nothing. My money was depleting rapidly, so I started selling drugs for old friends. Thank God for all the friends I made as a cop or I would have starved to death.

About three months later, I fell in love with the woman who would become my wife. I immediately had more children and fell in love with the family man way of life. My wife opened up all kinds of new doors for me. Two years later, with her advice I bought several houses and entered the real estate business.

One day while watching the news in my sixteen-room house, I heard that there was a serial killer in Atlantic City who was killing prostitutes. They said that at least four girls had been found in the swamp along Black Horse Pike. I called my contacts in Atlantic CIty to see if any of them had been identified. I was told that most were not, that they had been dead for so long. I learned the four girls were found in a drainage ditch behind a row of seedy motels. I also found out that all of the women were white. One might think that I was relieved. I was terribly saddened. No one deserves to die like that. No one!

I still find myself to this day talking to working girls whenever I get the chance. You see they are my people and I feel at home when I talk to them. I would like to ask anyone who reads

this book to understand that it is not easy being in the sporting life and feeling like the under

belly and scourge of society, all the while being at the beckoning call of society's demands.

Pimps and women of the night are reduced to the world's oldest profession for a multitude of

reasons and cling to each other because they all feel trapped in it. It is a constant pendulum

swing of feast and famine that could end at any moment.

Even those like myself who do not feel trapped in it tend to feel as though people in this

world see the world as they do and are aware that those who do not see the world as you do

either admirer you or hate you and, above all, they do not understand you. So that makes it sort

of a secret society. Anyone in the game will almost instantly recognize someone else who is or

has been in the game. You can see it in their face; you can feel it from the vibe that they give off.

Women on the street will say to me, "you know, you come off as a pimp to me", with me doing

my best to appear "normal". Even in prison, pimps gravitate toward each other. Pimping makes

you part of a special fraternity where everyone understands you and hot that makes you tick and

feel. Pimps have their own clothes, cars, homes, colors, music. They even have a dance and drive

a certain way. I have always wondered whether pimps were made or born; that is still debated in

certain corners of society. I believe it is a combination of both. I believe early socialization,

communication skills, self-confidence, and your relationship with your mother, as well as the

way you witnessed your mother deal with men, play the key roles.

Pimping can also be seen as a trade that can be used whenever times get hard. After I

pulled up out of Atlantic City and before I was married, I would meet a woman from time to time

who would complain about money and her bills. I would suggest Atlantic City. We would go down there for just the weekend and make at least five thousand dollars. A few times I even let

her keep all the money. Just being around the game was all the pay I needed.

Reflections

After looking back over my life and examining my mistakes, mishaps, and misfortunes, I

have some regrets. I wonder how things would have been had I not been agnostic, sometimes

atheist, sometimes downright evil. I wonder had I chosen another past; I would have been

happier, satisfied, secure, and wealthy, or maybe even one of "Gods" children? You see, when I

first started writing this book, I wanted to explain myself, hoping the reader would understand

why I lived the way I did…. and do. I wanted to leave something behind in the Library of

Congress for all eternity so that my four sons and their children could read it generations from now and understand me.

Crime is something people do out of necessity. Pimping is a "feeling," an emotion, a substitute Dopamine that gives you a "high" and the strength to operate in a society that has pimped you."

Throughout my life, I have used crime and pimping to combat the "establishment" as well as society at large. I have used pimping to empower me, and I have used drugs to weaken those more powerful than myself, thereby empowering me to pimp them. What people consider sick about me since I was a child was that I have enjoyed doing it. That is a sickness. I call it a sickness because, as long as everyone is of age and consenting in the state of Nevada, and Rhode Island, it is not a crime. But it is self-consuming, self-destroying and highly addictive, just like any other drug. It is especially addictive to a black man who has never felt any power.

Pimps are dedicated and steadfast to their trade because of their emotion toward the trade. A person who feels no hope and is starving to death will see the face of Jesus in the snow and become a "devout" Christian who could never be turned away from their faith. Well, the same thing happens to a pimp. In essence, the pimp game becomes his religion. He dresses the part, drives his car a certain way, and, most importantly, lives by the pimp code and rules, or at least tries his best to do so. The feeling of being a pimp comes on gradually. It seeps into your being and never leaves, creating a desire to strengthen or tighten up your game. It is more the same way a Christian who is always looking to get closer to Christ.

In this stage of my life I am not pimping. I am married with four sons. I know that some pimp is reading this right now and saying: "What the hell does that have to do with anything?" Real pimps are going to pimp regardless. I had to switch gears; my brains desire very much to pimp right now. It is just not conducive to my lifestyle. I am with my children a lot. I also have a

newborn. Although I love pimping, it is a very difficult trade, as well as time consuming. I am

also aware being difficult is what makes the men that do it great! I have had to settle for the

"Brooklyn Hustle". I have to be versatile when it comes to crime. Pimps are "specialist" one

dimensional with mouths to feed and tuition, mortgages, property taxes, car notes, and utilities to

pay. I have been forced to be a scavenger, an all around criminal with a digestive system that can

digest bones and hair, not just meat.

I was recently asked by someone if I had "learned my lesson?" given all that I had been

through. I was asked this question while posing for a magazine cover entitled "AS IS" magazine.

I was taken back for a minute.

The only way for me to feel regret or to have learned a lesson would be to have never

been born black in the first place.

I never had a choice. It was either starve or do crime. Every black child in the ghetto who

embarks on a life of crime follow behind the men whom he most respects and admires. Those

men become a sort of a father figure to that young man who will do all that he can to emulate.

Pimping has always been special to me. It's the street hustle that requires the most

dedication and discipline. It also has the most perks.

The best way to steer a young boy away from pimping is to change his environment. If a

young boy is starving, living without heat in his house, with no real men around him, guess what

he's going to take when he sees the first person who he deems best fit to survive in his dismal

circumstances? And believe you, me that will not be a law abiding citizen.

All of my children go to private schools and are the only black children in their classes.

It's not out of self hatred, quite the contrary. I teach my children to love being black, but white

people are the best equipped to survive in this society. So I want my children to learn from them

and not to emulate them.

I have been ranked as the third most corrupt police officer in the history of the N.Y.P.D.

It seems notorious and scary, but it is far from true. The most corrupt cops do not become police

commissioners or each appointed rank up to Captain, because up until that rank there is a Civil

Exam. Deputy Inspector, Inspector, Deputy Chief (one star), Bureau Chief (two stars), Assistant

Chief (three stars), Chief of Department (four stars) and Police Commissioner (five stars) are all

assigned posts. This means it is given to you regardless of education, know how, or merit. An

example of this is Bernard Kerik who never passed a promotional exam. As a police officer, he

was awarded the rank of Commissioner of the corrections department. Then he was awarded the

rank of Police Commissioner. Bernard Kerik is now inmate number 84888-054 at Cumberland

Federal Correctional Institution. Now that is a corrupt cop. I was just a nigger getting by, and

believe it or not, he is ranked below me. Above me, are Michael Dowd of the "Dowd Crew" (7-

5 PCT) in East New York, Brooklyn and Crystal Spivey of the notorious "Buddy Boy's" of the

7-7 PCT also in Brooklyn.

While being interviewed by Vernon and Shanica Garrison for the blog talk radio show

"Apples and Peaches", I was asked about destroying the African American community? I replied

that it had been destroyed long before I got there. Right now, due to the Gulf of Mexico spill,

sharks are coming closer to the shore than ever before, eating any and everything to survive

because the establishment has taken away the food it needs to survive because of off shore

drilling. Would you blame the shark for destroying life in the ocean? So how can you blame me?

My family and I are gonna survive if we have to resort to cannibalism. I will just season the meat so they won't know it… L.O.L. that really what I have always done in a way… anyway.

One would argue that I did have a choice, that I could have just been a cop for twenty years, barely getting by, and retire at 40 with a bad back. Not me. I am not going to be just another nigger. Neither will my children. I feel the same way that Joseph Kennedy one of my favorite criminals felt. He did crime in an intelligent manner and his son went on to become President. The Kennedys are part of the upper echelon of power and wealth in this country. All of it was built on the back of a criminal from an impoverished neighborhood. That is how I see my family in years to come. The reason that family has had so many problems is because they forgot that they were criminals.

We Gourdines will never have that problem. Although I had to be, my children and their children will not be. Gourdine is old French for "whore". I see the origin of the word as a constant reminder.

I have also been asked if I would recommend that a young man, pimp or sell drugs. There are opportunities out there, but I would say to use it as a last resort, not a first one. This country was founded by criminals, but I cater to those who are not.

I have lost a lot of people along the way. I owe each and every one of them for any success I have experienced. They are people who have stood by me in the toughest of times. Recently, I was driving down Pacific Avenue in Atlantic City, in my magnificent ho catching chariot (that's a car to you readers), when I saw Carmen from New York. I called her over to the car and she stunk so bad that she burned the hairs in my nose. I ignored it and told her to get in. She started off trying to apologizes for pimping me as a teen…and for trying to kill me. I asked her why she apologizes for pimping me first. She looked away with tears in her eyes, trying to

fix herself up as best as she could. Her hair is matted; her skin looked awful; her teeth were

jagged and yellow with a thick layer of tarter at the gums. Her eyes were yellow like her teeth,

which suggested she had Hepatitis C. Her nails, once magnificent, were blackened like a dead

woman's. So was her toe in her open toe mix-matched shoes.

"Mickman" I'm dying from Aids and Hepatitis C," Carmen said. "I sleep in the street and

eat out of garbage cans." To sell someone is a slow death, but by having you shot you would

have for sure never lived like I'm living now.

I'm watching myself die more and more every day. I told her that I never took it personal.

It was a learning experience and that we were both victims of our society and our time as kids. I

hugged her and kissed her on the cheek. I gave her all the money I had on me, which was six

hundred and twenty-five dollars. Good Luck Carmen, You will always be special to me.

Pimps and career criminals are different from the common people in another respect. We

are very generous; in fact, the most abused people usually are. We always know that things could

be completely different. Next year, I could be sitting in Carmen's seat. If I don't keep my heart

cold and my survival instinct firm, focused and clear as crystal. But, I know, I will be.

Acknowledgments

To my wife, my children, everyone named in this book, my barber Hex from Union County, New Jersey *(who was the first person to read anything I wrote)*, my niece, Jiana Leshay Barns, Jamilla Vasser Buie and to everyone in the game.

I want to thank the man who inspired me as a child, and made this book possible. Lorenzo "Fat Cat" Nichols.

The following people have been my hope, guiding light and friends without them this also would not have happened:

Uncle Perry Burns, Carmen Nieves, Jamiala Mack, ,Calice Romicka Buie, Capalitana Micronia Buie, Eric D. Heckstall and thank you Dron J. Chepesiuk and Stratetgic Media Books for making this book literate.

Made in the USA
Columbia, SC
01 February 2023

11441879R00085